The Compliance Entrepreneur's Handbook

TOOLS, TIPS, AND TACTICS TO FIND YOUR KILLER
IDEA AND CREATE SUCCESS ON YOUR OWN TERMS

Kristy Grant-Hart
Kristen Liston
Joseph E. Murphy

BRENTHAM HOUSE PUBLISHING
Covent Garden, London

Brentham House
Publishing Company Ltd.
COVENT GARDEN

The Compliance Entrepreneur's Handbook: Tools, Tips, and Tactics to Find Your Killer Idea and Create Success on Your Own Terms.

Copyright © 2021 by Kristy Grant-Hart, Kirsten Liston, and Joseph E. Murphy.

Brentham House Publishing Company
71-75 Shelton Street
Covent Garden
London, WC2H 9JQ

Brentham House Publishing Company books may be purchased for educational, business or sales promotional use. For information, please email the Special Markets Department at Info@BrenthamHouse.com.

FIRST EDITION

A CIP Record of this book is available from the British Library.
ISBN: 978-0-9934788-9-5 (soft cover edition)
ISBN: 978-1-5272-9188-1 (electronic edition)

Brentham House
Publishing Company Ltd.
COVENT GARDEN

"What happens when Kristy Grant-Hart, Joe Murphy and Kristen Liston collaborate? One of the best books for every compliance professional. _The Compliance Entrepreneur's Handbook_ is a must-read for everyone in the compliance profession; from the long-time CCO to the one-month compliance newbie. Packed with tales, stories and anecdotes; if you have ever thought about starting a compliance business or simply building your compliance brand, this is the book for you. I wish it had been around when I started my compliance business but I will use it going forward."

- _Tom Fox, the Compliance Evangelist and founder of the Compliance Podcast Network_

"_The Compliance Entrepreneur's Handbook_ is an engaging and compelling read, authored by three of the most successful entrepreneurs in the ethics and compliance field. The handbook offers practical advice, insights and a road map to success for anyone working in the field – from professionals just starting out to seasoned compliance veterans – who have an original idea and dream of starting a compliance or ethics business of their own. Get a copy of this book and read it today!"

- _Kirk Jordan, co-founder, Integrity Interactive_

"Taking a career step from having a corporate role to starting your own business is as exciting as it is intimidating! In _The Compliance Entrepreneur's Handbook_, Kristy, Joe and Kirsten break down the 'before, during and after' steps into actionable nuggets of wisdom and experience, as to bring you on an end-to-end journey of entrepreneurship. Right in the introduction, they address what's often the most daunting question of "where to start," which, as they well point out, is well before "you step out on your own." So get out plenty of highlighters, post-its and notepads as to take a road map developed by three thought leaders in the field and to make it your own!"

- *Richard Bistrong, CEO, Front-Line Anti-Bribery LLC*

"Warning: this book will make you want to turn that entrepreneur dream into a reality. I couldn't put it down. At every turn it felt like Kristy, Kirsten and Joseph were reaching out a hand, willing me to succeed and cheering me on as I started to formulate my path for success!"

- Laura Ellis, Global Ethics and Compliance Manager, Cisco

"Every new entrepreneur knows the grim statistic that 50% of businesses with employees fail in the first five years. They also know that 100% of the people who learn they are a new entrepreneur will give them business advice (whether they ask for it or not), and so they need to be shrewd in choosing to whom they will listen. The authors of *The Compliance Entrepreneur's Handbook* are among the few who have beaten the odds and established successful ventures in the compliance industry, and they've filled this book with practical, actionable, and relatable advice you can use to map out your own journey."

- Ricardo Pellafone, founder, The Broadcat

Contents

To Lisa Hall and Megan Tepper, who gave me the gift of courage through their unwavering belief in my dreams.

— Kristy Grant-Hart

To Patti Caswell and Andrea Falcione — I am grateful for the passion, drive, camaraderie, candor, and ridiculous levels of talent you bring to this shared enterprise of ours. Who knew it could be this much fun?

— Kirsten Liston

To the compliance and ethics professionals around the world whose daily, tireless commitment to doing the right thing makes all the difference.

— Joe Murphy

Foreword
by Ben Di Pietro

The world changed a lot the past 10 years, and based on what is happening today we can expect it to look drastically different 10 years from now.

While many will read that and become anxious over what the future will hold, the entrepreneurs out there will leap into action, seeing opportunity in the uncertainty, sensing the chance to make something great, to build a business that has meaning and which will positively impact people and how they live.

This certainly will be true in the ethics and compliance (E&C) space. Increased emphasis on building values-based cultures founded upon the principles of moral leadership, diversity, equity, inclusion, truth and transparency is critical for successful businesses looking to attract top talent and keep their customers satisfied.

As new technologies, and new twists on old technologies, alter the way we live, work, and interact, E&C teams will be reacting, responding and trying to get in front of the forces shaping how we work, when we work, and where we work.

As I have watched this profession grow from an afterthought to a leading member of the business leadership team at some of the world's most successful and profitable companies, the need to provide E&C teams with professional, sophisticated and nuanced help has led to an explosion of new companies offering everything from training and communications, to helping navigate the world of regulations, to helping to build cultures that emphasize ethics as a normal part of the decision-making process.

These E&C teams will get help from the people who take the chance to take an idea from their mind and put it into the world, to build a product or service from their thoughts that will help people work better, smarter, more efficiently.

These entrepreneurs won't stop until they have funding to build their dreams, until they find the right people to join them on the journey, until they not only create their product or service, but get it to the people who can most benefit from it.

In the end, entrepreneurs do. They find solutions to their problems, climb over, under or around their hurdles, cultivate relationships to help them take a "no," or an "I'm not sure," and turn it into a "yes, I'm with you."

It's that refusal to take no for an answer that separates entrepreneurs who succeed from those who don't.

You will find in this book everything you need to know about how to get an E&C business started, how to get it funded, and what to think about when putting a business plan together and building a team. Kristy, Kirsten, and Joe use the stories of their own experiences to map a road for how to get a company off and running, how to grow it, when to grow it, and most importantly, how to sell it and when to sell it.

There are plenty of books out there with tips on how to become an entrepreneur; none that I know of is specific to the ethics and compliance field, of how to be successful in this profession, with advice from three of the leading minds in the industry, all of whom have achieved entrepreneurial success in the E&C space.

Each of the authors shares their own story of overcoming fears and taking the plunge to become an entrepreneur, of those nervous nights awake in bed wondering if they made the right decision. Their stories show how they overcame challenges, stayed encouraged when others would become discouraged, and never were afraid to take a chance if the rewards outweighed the risks.

Another important lesson from their personal stories: Don't become content. Kristy, Kirsten, and Joe all have found areas outside of E&C for them to expand their entrepreneurial activities. As they grew more confident, they were willing to push themselves into new areas where success wasn't guaranteed. But knowing they did it before was all they needed to know they could do it again.

While this book has much to offer, what this book can't provide you is the drive, the will and the determination to make your dream happen. No entrepreneur can succeed without that; the desire only can come from within.

And the commitment to the mission must be complete. As the book sagely states, "Some people choose to place a toe in the water, but our advice is to go all-in, at least emotionally. If you choose to take the entrepreneurial plunge, it will be easier to stay committed if you start committed. The journey is too difficult for people who allow themselves to easily waver."

Those words are lingering with me because, as I write this, I find myself in a period of transition: in between jobs, approaching 60 years old, thinking about how I want the next chapter of my life to unfold. I've always been flush with ideas, but unsure if the work to bring those ideas to life is worth the stress and uncertainty.

I write this because, if you are debating whether to become an entrepreneur, you have to know yourself, who you are, what you want. Are you a person who will fight through adversity, and then do it again, and again? Can you pick yourself up when you fall, and jump back in with the same level of commitment? How much do you want it?

My experience in life is people who want something more than other people tend to get that thing, because they are more driven, because they don't give up when times get tough, when obstacles repel others who are unsure of their commitment, unsure of whether the time, effort and investment is justified.

You can digest all the great advice this book has to offer, but if you don't want it more than everyone else, you won't achieve the success you desire.

But if you have the want to, this book shares the know-how to get you there.

- Ben DiPietro

Ben DiPietro is a leader in ethics, compliance, corporate culture, and crisis management, with more than three decades of experience in journalism. During his career, he worked at The Wall Street Journal, where he helped to launch its Risk & Compliance Journal and the 'Crisis of the Week' column, and was an Associated Press newsman in Oregon and Hawaii.

CHAPTER 1

Introduction

You're here because you have a dream: being your own boss. Choosing your own hours. Picking the projects you want to work on. Going on vacation without asking for permission from your unhelpful employer. Escaping the watercooler and the gossip that takes place around it. Determining how much money you make instead of waiting for the measly 2% raise being offered this year. You're ready to abandon the steady paycheck in favor of building something great. No – you're happy to abandon the steady paycheck in favor of building something great that is yours. You're ready to go out on your own and start your business.

Congratulations – you've come to the right place. In this book, we're going to give you all the information we wish we knew when we started on our entrepreneurial journeys. From raising capital to selling the business, we're here to guide you on the path to success. We'll share the secrets of creating a great company and in-demand products and services. We'll guide you towards the inside track to help make your entrepreneurial dreams come true.

We wrote this book because while there are great books written about entrepreneurship, there weren't any available specifically about starting a business in the compliance and ethics industry. We realized this in 2020 when we co-presented a discussion at the Society of Corporate Compliance and Ethics' national conference on creating a business in the compliance and ethics field. On our first call, we talked for more than an hour about the myriad topics we wanted to cover. "We should write a book!" exclaimed Joe, and from there we were off to the races.

This book is a labor of love for the three authors – Joe Murphy, Kirsten Liston, and Kristy Grant-Hart. It's full of our best advice and contains step-by-step guidance to create a wildly successful business in the field.

How This Book Will Help You

This book is intended to shepherd you from the inception of your dream through the sale of your business. It's divided into four sections. Each one builds on the last to help you triumph in enterprise.

Section One

The first section details what you should do before you step out on your own. It includes advice on what to complete while you're still in-house to prepare to launch your business. It goes into detail about determining what your business does and how to find a great niche for your product or service.

Next, you'll learn how to choose your business model. Getting this right before you start can save you tremendous headaches later.

This section also contains information on partnership, advisors, giving up equity (or keeping it all), and strategic alliances. Lastly, we'll go into financing your big dream and finding capital.

Section Two

The second section is all about execution – what to do now that you're ready to start. It begins with the basics of where to work and how to structure your days. Then it goes into the most critical aspect of a business – sales. Without sales, there is no business, so learning how to make sales and build market demand is critical.

Section Three

The third section is about marketing. Without marketing, no one will know about your business. Here we give you step-by-step guidance to raise your voice above the noise. We go into how to successfully write and speak your way into fame in the industry – and get paid to do it.

We'll go into building your brand presence online, including how to use free tools and social media to catapult you on to the digital scene. Then we'll talk about how to network for entrepreneurial success. Hint – it's not the same as networking while you're in-house.

Section Four

The last section deals with exit strategy – planning to sell the business – or not. As you'll learn, thinking from the end is one of the hallmarks of a highly successful business, so planning properly now can pay massive dividends at the end.

Who Are We?

Why should you take advice from us? We've practiced what we preach, and each of us has a successful business in the compliance and ethics field. Each of our businesses has a different focus and way of executing. Each of our businesses has evolved in ways we didn't anticipate, and they're still growing today. We hope that you identify with the journeys we've been on – our successes and failures – so that you come out better informed and ready to thrive.

Here are our stories.

Kristy's Entrepreneur Story

"Hold on! This book says there's another way into the Screen Actors Guild! You can start your own production company, register as a producer with the guild, then find a project, then submit yourself as an actor into the union! This is so great!" The other extras on the set of the TV show stared at me like I was crazy. Why would you start your own company so you could be a professional actor?

I'd been acting my whole life. Since the age of five, playing an angel in the church play, I'd been absolutely hooked. I followed that passion and eventually was accepted into the film and theatre school at UCLA.

When I graduated, I was ready to act professionally; but to do so on any of the big TV shows, I had to be admitted into the Screen Actors Guild. Other than being discovered at a coffee shop, the only way in I'd heard to do this was to be an extra on film and TV sets. Each day the first assistant director had magic tickets to give to a couple of the extras. If you managed to collect three magic tickets, you could join the guild. However, that typically took months, and for some people, it simply never happened. I didn't want to slog through long days on set making minimum wage to get to my dream. One day, while trying to solve the problem, I found my answer. On the last page of a book on acting, there were two paragraphs dedicated to starting a company – the backdoor route into the guild.

That night I began my research, which led to the creation of my first company, Uplifting Pictures, which was dedicated to making travel and tourism-related shows. I convinced the shipowner of the riverboat where I sang on weekends to let me film a commercial for their dinner cruise. I named myself producer of the commercial, starred in it, and filled out the producer's paperwork admitting myself into the Screen Actors Guild. I went on to do several commercials for companies like eBay and AT&T and had small TV roles, including one on *Unsolved Mysteries*.

Everything Changes

One fateful night, as I was growing weary of the constant insecurity of the acting world, some friends rented the movie *Legally Blonde*. As the movie ended, my friend asked me what I thought of the film. I got highly emotional and said, "I loved it. I think I should go to law school!" When I told my mother that I'd decided to go back to school, she candidly replied, "You can't go to law school, you're an actress." Nevertheless, I pursued the path, and she came around, ultimately becoming my biggest cheerleader. I got a job as a legal secretary and put myself through four long years of night law school, working full time during the day, going to four hours of classes at night, then studying all weekend. All that work paid off, as I ultimately graduated *summa cum laude* from Loyola Law School.

Compliance Calls

I joined the law firm of Gibson, Dunn & Crutcher out of law school. After looking around, I chose to join the Foreign Corrupt Practices Act (FCPA) group because the lawyers in that practice traveled extensively, and I wanted to see the world. I worked on corporate monitorships, including the Siemens monitorship, which at the time represented the largest bribery fine in history. In 2011, Gibson Dunn sent me to London to work on a banking scandal. I flew between London and Switzerland for months performing the investigation. I also went online dating, and, to my surprise, met Jonathan, a darling British man who would become my husband.

I knew I'd have to change gears to stay in Britain, as I didn't have the ability to practice law there. I went to see a recruiter. He told me I should consider compliance since I had anti-bribery, antitrust, and data privacy experience. I agreed. I became the Director of Compliance for Europe, the Middle East, and Africa for Carlson Wagonlit Travel.

A year later I received a call from the headhunter at NBCUniversal. They wanted me to consider joining their joint venture with Paramount Pictures as the chief compliance officer. When I asked why they'd chosen me, they said I was the only person they could find with compliance experience and a film degree.

I loved my job. As I grew in the profession and attended conferences, I saw that many compliance officers struggled with influence and persuasion in the companies where they worked. I believed I had something unique to say within the compliance profession, as I had studied sales techniques and storytelling. I wanted to help my compliance friends who hadn't had experience and training in those techniques. I began writing what would become my first book, *How to Be a Wildly Effective Compliance Officer*.[1]

Brentham House Publishing Company

Compliance is a highly niche specialty, so I knew that publication by the major publishing houses was a non-starter. I began listening to podcasts for authors. In one episode, an author was interviewed who had started his own publishing company. He explained that traditional publishers only paid 10% royalties, plus they had complete control of the book's cover, title, materials, etc. Major publishers usually don't pay for marketing anymore unless they expect the book to be a national best seller. He was frustrated by that. He also didn't want to go down the publish-on-Amazon route, because he couldn't sell his book through bookstores and couldn't easily sell them to libraries if they were self-published. His response was to start his own publishing company.

Starting a publishing house sounded perfect to me. I created a limited company and went about learning all the ins and outs of the publishing world. I chose the name Brentham House Publishing Company because I lived in the Brentham Garden Estate area of London, and "house" related to publishing houses. It took me a year to complete *Wildly Effective* and to have Brentham House Publishing Company ready to launch. On Feb. 4, 2016, *How to Be a Wildly Effective Compliance Officer* was published. I held a launch party at Daunt Books in Central London and had a photographer come to take pictures.

I knew the book needed publicity, so I contacted Ben DiPietro at the *Wall Street Journal* and sent him a copy of my book. To my astonishment, he did a feature piece and interview with me in the risk and compliance section of the paper. I sent the book to every thought leader and publication in the compliance field. The book became a hit. Brentham House would later publish several more of my books, then expand to publishing other author's books, including Patrick O'Kane's *Fix it Fast: GDPR*.

Brentham House books are now sold on Amazon globally, as well as in bookstores. Copies of many of the books are in libraries, including the British Library, Oxford College Library, the National Library of Scotland, the National Library of Wales, and at Trinity College in Dublin.

Starting Spark Compliance Consulting

When I went into law, I wanted to be a partner at Gibson Dunn. When that door closed because I stayed in England longer than the firm needed me there, I still longed to have multiple clients and to be working on several projects at a time. I knew that starting a compliance consultancy was risky. I also knew from my film and television days that there is nothing like publicity to propel a new venture and that *Wildly Effective* would likely create that for me. I decided to take the plunge, starting both the publishing house and creating the consulting company at the same time.

My contract at United International Pictures had a six-month notice period, which was a great gift to me. I turned in my resignation in July 2015 and told the management that I would be starting a consulting company after my notice period was complete. During those six months, I began to prepare in earnest. I knew I had skills in the compliance profession, but I did not know how to run a business.

Getting my first few clients was nerve-wracking. The first month I was in business, I went to get advice from an American lawyer acquaintance of mine who worked in a big law firm in the anti-bribery practice. I'll never forget him saying to me, "Kristy, I've been here a few years now. It's almost impossible to build a career in London in law or compliance as an American. It's doubly-impossible to do so as a woman. I'd recommend you go back in-house while you still can." To this day, I don't think he meant to be sexist or condescending. I think he believed what he was saying. Still, it unnerved me. It also fueled my passion to prove him and every other naysayer wrong.

Expanding

Three months after starting Spark Compliance, a friend of mine from my Gibson Dunn days contacted me. She had completed a master's course in compliance and was interested in joining me at Spark. I wanted to capitalize on my large network in the States, so she joined Spark Compliance as a partner. Jonathan, my husband, joined as a partner six months later, as we became busier and busier and needed help running the financial/accounting side of the business. We later expanded into Atlanta and, most recently, New York.

I worked hard on the marketing side. I created my one-minute weekly video, the "Wildly Effective Compliance Officer Tip of the Week." I began to blog every week and offered to do any webinar, podcast, speaking performance, or writing I could. I developed a reputation, and by the end of my first year in business, I was regularly performing paid keynote speeches on my book topics. It had all come full circle. I used to perform monologues as an actress. I was now performing paid, hour-long monologues in front of thousands of people. Earlier in my life I never would have guessed my performance on stage would be about compliance!

The Next Entrepreneurial Adventure

I love being an entrepreneur, and my entrepreneurial journey continues to expand year on year. Once you've caught the business bug, entrepreneurial opportunity can strike in unexpected ways.

For instance, in 2018, Jonathan and I visited the New River Gorge area of West Virginia. It's home to the best white water rafting on the East Coast, along with world-class climbing and hiking trails. We thought there was a great deal of opportunity in tourism there, so in 2019, we began the journey to purchase 12 cabins on 38 acres in the area. The process of acquiring the vacation rentals business put us in front of groups of bankers, pitching why we were qualified to take it over, and how we would make it more profitable. I had no idea how to obtain commercial loans or how to value an existing business, but I had worked in tourism previously at Carlson Wagonlit Travel, as well as stints at hotels and airlines prior to law school. I believed we could do it.

On April 11, 2019, we closed on the property and began the journey of owning a new venture. Jonathan took over running Carnifex Ferry Cabins, as well as continuing his work with Spark. During our first year of ownership, we installed an online booking system, put the cabins on Airbnb, added all new linen, hired a calling service to answer the phones, and launched social media for the site. We were up 20% that summer and 40% in the off-season.

The area was recently designated a national park, which has created incredible demand.

What's Next?

When the COVID-19 crisis hit, I knew I would need to pivot. I couldn't perform paid speaking engagements in a lockdown, and traveling back and forth from Europe to West Virginia and California would have to stop for a while. I decided to start filming online classes. Jonathan and I set up a film studio at our house, and we began to film and edit numerous classes. Once again, that film and television background came into play. It's amazing to me how much of life comes full circle.

In addition to launching the online classes, we began working on creating software for the compliance field. Jonathan and I continue to look at properties to purchase and develop. My ultimate goal is to be an investor in female entrepreneurship, especially in the technology space. I want to give back and lift up women brave enough to choose the entrepreneurial route.

Five years before I started Spark Compliance, a close friend of mine went to culinary school. When she graduated, she started her own successful meal preparation service. During that time, she said to me something I have never forgotten. It was, "When you learn that you can make your own money without a job, you'll never go back." For me, that has been true, and I hope it always will be. I love being a business owner. I love working with other entrepreneurs. I love my employees fiercely and appreciate everything that they do. I hope that I am always able to build businesses, both in the compliance world and beyond.

Joe's Entrepreneur Story

I started on the route to compliance and ethics in 1976 as a young lawyer doing antitrust work in-house. I was at AT&T, the old Bell Telephone System, which, at the time, was the world's largest corporation. At that moment, we were just seeing the entrance of competitors into the American telecommunications market. Previously, Bell had a legal and regulated monopoly, but that was now being opened up. The difficulty was that for any competitor to reach a customer, it had to rely on the Bell local facilities. Obviously this created tension. To address this challenge, the Bell companies created contact and liaison groups whose job was to ensure competitors had this access and that it was done fairly.

In the part of Bell where I worked, I was the antitrust lawyer and thus became the lawyer for the company employees who were in this competitor liaison group. I remember one of the liaison offices dealt with competitive equipment vendors. Initially, the office was staffed by an engineer whose nickname happened to be "Mr. Clean." Thereafter that became the accepted name for the office.

We had separate groups that dealt with long-distance competitors and also competitive suppliers. From this, I learned that you could actually have groups in a company whose orientation was not simply selling to customers, but being fair to competitors. In other words, they were a constituency dedicated to doing the right thing. This was the basis for my realizing that companies were not simply black boxes and that these internal groups could make a difference, but they needed strong support for this to happen.

Compliance in the Crosshairs

To ensure that the telephone operating companies were doing the right thing, people from the corporate headquarters were sent out to review the subsidiaries' operations. They produced reports critiquing the operations and made recommendations for how the subsidiary could work more effectively with competitors.

In 1982, the US government brought an antitrust case against AT&T to break it up. The reports were obtained by the government during discovery and used against the company. The message was clear: Companies should avoid carrying out these types of internal reviews because they would become evidence against them.

The frustration with this was fueling the development of a new idea called the "self-evaluative privilege." The doctrine stated that if a company performs internal reviews to prevent misconduct, the product of that review should not be used against the company. I began reading everything I could find on the topic. I found just one case, but couldn't find any articles, only student notes. I published the first article on the topic in the *Journal of Corporation Law*.

Subsequently, I wrote other pieces developing this concept. As a result of this and speaking on the self-evaluative privilege, I started to develop a following.

Publishing – and Selling – a Book

When I was an undergraduate, I was lucky to study under the distinguished professor Jay Sigler at Rutgers University. Jay had been my mentor during college, and throughout the years, we remained in touch. I remember at one lunch at the Latham Hotel, Jay looked at me and said, "It's time we did a book together." I, of course, thought that was a great idea. Jay called his publisher, explained the project, and they said, "When can you get it to us?"

Jay and I wrote our first book having dinners at his place in Philadelphia on one weekday evening each week, while his wife, Janet, could critique our writing. We were so in the flow that, at the end of each evening, we had lots of ideas but neither one of us could say exactly where each idea came from. Our book, *Interactive Corporate Compliance*, was the first book on the topic of compliance and ethics ever published.

Finding a Business Partner and Launching the First Venture

After the book was published, I was invited to a program through the University of Denver School of Law. Under the direction of Ed Dauer, the school's National Center for Preventive Law was creating a restatement of the law and principles of compliance. It was there I met Kirk Jordan. Kirk had been a lawyer at Skadden Arps but went out on his own to found the first law firm dedicated to corporate compliance. Kirk and I were each committee heads on the project.

After our meeting in Denver, Kirk called to ask if he could meet with me and get advice for work he was doing for a major corporate client. I got permission from my boss and took the time off to do this. Amazingly, I got paid $400 just to have lunch (and this was in the early '90s)!

When I reached the point where I was ready to take the leap and go out "on my own," Kirk was the person I decided to work with. We named our enterprise Compliance Systems Legal Group (CSLG). Although he was in Rhode Island and I was in South Jersey, that never seemed to matter. After all, clients expected us to go to them, and Kirk and I were able to keep in contact regularly.

CSLG specialized in computer-based compliance training. At the time this was done on kiosks using physical media, such as disks. It was a fun but slow process to develop materials for clients. We worked closely with a company called VIS that specialized in this type of technology.

One of our close associates at VIS was Carl Nelson. Carl knew how difficult it was to work with companies on developing customized training, and how one could spend forever with a company's human resources staff and not get anything finalized. He knew the key was to have a product that could be shared among different companies, allowing some customizing but with enough consistency that one could start the training in a relatively brief time.

The Internet Changes Everything

One day in 1998, Kirk called to ask if I was interested in forming a new company. Kirk had been watching the development of the internet with great interest. He believed that compliance training delivered by the internet could be a huge hit. I was all for it. We formed our next company, Integrity International.

Kirk was smart about business – he said we were lawyers, not business managers. In our little company, Kirk and I did not feel that we needed to be experts. Instead, we teamed up with an expert. We knew the man to call – Carl Nelson from VIS.

We knew from experience that starting up a company was Carl's forte. He told us that it was fun until you reached about a hundred employees and then it was time to sell. He had done this before, and we understood that he knew what he was doing.

Remarkably, Kirk recommended that Carl run things. While Kirk and I would own the business with Carl, Carl would be our boss. It takes a great deal of humility to recognize what Kirk recognized. Carl's business acumen proved invaluable. The end goal was always to build and then sell the business. Carl operated with the end in mind. He knew when to hire new salespeople: revenue might not have covered their costs initially, but he knew that it eventually would.

Financing the Dream

One immediate question was how to get the capital we needed to properly launch Integrity International. As we were mulling over options, I got a call from Jim Seidl, whom I had known for years through my compliance activities. He and his company, Legal Research Center (LRC), were looking for a place to invest in the emerging online training field. I said that yes, I did know of such a company because we were creating it. His words to me were "that's why I called you."

We had Jim come to our Dedham, Massachusetts headquarters to visit and check us out. Very soon after that, we had our first and only major investment. His company put $500,000 into our business and got a ton of stock as a result. Without question that would have seemed highly risky, but it turned out to be a brilliant investment for Jim and his company. When Integrity Interactive sold, he gave bonuses to every person in his company.

When we got our $500,000 investor, we definitely had to give up a big percentage. But I had already accepted the idea that a small percentage of a big amount was better than a giant percentage of a tiny amount. We also gave options to our productive people, and it was the same principle. It was another example of those starting the business opting for a smaller piece of something bigger by sharing with teammates.

Taking It to the Next Level: Private Equity

After a few years of growth and successful operation, we hired a search firm and had several private equity groups interested in investing in Integrity. After much back and forth, one was willing to pay our price for a majority share of the ownership. We sold with escrows that were released afterward when we hit certain benchmarks. We hit them all, so there were later payouts as well.

Ultimately, the private equity investment fund found a buyer for all of the shares, and Integrity International was no longer ours. We had done it. We had created the company, built it, found investment, and then successfully sold the business.

Kirsten's Entrepreneur Story

I started in compliance in September of 2000. I'd just moved across the country to take a job with Integrity International, a small start-up that was inventing the brand-new field of online compliance learning.

So I was alarmed when, at my first company meeting, the CEO of Integrity casually mentioned that the company had no customers, no contracts, and no revenue. (*What? Why hadn't I asked that in the interview!? I was just a journalist looking for a stable paycheck!*)

These were the dot-com days, the internet gold rush. For every one person who took a cafeteria job at Amazon and became a millionaire, a thousand more joined a company like Pets.com only to go down with the ship. In my case, the ship called Integrity Interactive turned out to be seaworthy. But getting to that point was a journey on its own.

Writing as a Way of Life

True story: I actually first took the job at Integrity so I could free up time to write.

I came to this decision when I was in my first (and only) newspaper staff role, editing the calendar section of the local arts weekly. Most of my time was spent maintaining a giant database of every art and cultural event happening in the city (which I typed in from the hundreds of press releases I was sent every day.)

I also edited a small section called "The A-List," where the paper high-lighted about 20 events per week.

If an event made the A-List, it almost guaranteed a higher turnout (which meant I could get free tickets to anything I wanted to attend, a great perk for a 26 year old.) And because the A-List covered events in a range of dif-ferent areas— music, theater, visual art, literature, fashion, dance, street fairs — I had a roster of freelancers who could write an informed blurb about each event or performance.

Over time, I noticed something interesting: The freelancers who were happiest had another job — like a lawyer who wrote about dance. The dedi-cated writers seemed the least happy.

So I resolved to get a corporate job, one that would give me the brain space to be creative outside of work. This is the path that led me to Integrity.

Joining the Integrity Ship of Dreams

Within days of joining Integrity, I flew down to Virginia with Kirk Jordan, one of the company founders, where our first client signed our first contract and we kicked off a code of conduct course.

It was an early lesson in the kind of vision, market insight, and sheer be-lief you need to start a company — grounded and informed enough that you're not delusional; optimistic enough that you're willing to get out ahead of the money, especially if there are competitors in the mix.

A Front-Row Seat in a Growing Field

My early years at Integrity were more fun than I thought work could ever be.

Part of it was that the management team had a talent for building a cul-ture where people enjoyed and respected one another; where we worked hard (it's a lot of work to get a company off the ground!) but took time for fun and camaraderie.

But also, compliance turned out to be genuinely interesting – full of the same kinds of human problems and dilemmas that had attracted me to writing in the first place. Here, Joe Murphy was a big inspiration and influence, as it's not hard to get interested in compliance when Joe talks about it!

At first, company growth was slow. With the Sentencing Guidelines in place, most large companies knew they had to get serious about building a compliance program at some point – but most appeared to want to put it off if they could.

All this changed when Enron collapsed in 2001, followed by the Tyco, WorldCom, HealthSouth, and other corporate accounting scandals. Congress responded by passing the Sarbanes-Oxley Act, the most sweeping set of new business regulations since the 1930s.

I still remember the day the Enron news broke. Our company president was an early eBay power user — our office was full of desks and chairs he'd bought at auction, some still stacked up in empty offices in anticipation of rapid growth. As we digested the information hitting the newswire, he suddenly spotted Enron tchotchkes for sale. And not just any tchotchkes — people were selling ethics and compliance swag, Lucite "Respect. Integrity. Communication. Excellence" desk accessories and values posters they'd ripped off the walls on their way out the door.

We often told the Enron tchotchke story to the new companies signing up to illustrate why that needed to get serious about their compliance programs.

For several years afterward, sales were less of a challenge than managing growth. I remember walking into my manager's office one day with a list of 27 courses I was supposed to have written already. We built a larger team pretty quickly after that.

Integrity went on to attract hundreds of global customers. Mostly, we served Fortune 500 or Global 2000 companies, the same brands that ran Super Bowl ads or made the products I'd had in my cabinets for years. The courses I wrote were deployed to millions and then tens of millions of employees globally, in more than 60 languages. We had to figure out how to record audio in Spanish, then dozens more languages. Client services had to troubleshoot issues like the slow pace of internet bandwidth in Cameroon. The scale of it all was hard to fathom sometimes.

At the time, I was still learning the basics of building a career — how to hire and manage; how to be managed; how to set yourself up for the next step forward. So I was lucky to work at a company whose founders had started companies before and understood the phases a company passes through.

As we grew, our president Carl Nelson clearly articulated what was happening — what stage the company was going through, what we needed to focus on.

For instance, I remember him telling us at an all-hands meeting that all growing companies need to worry about working capital — funding the work before you get paid for the work. This concept, like so many others, came in handy when I found myself in the same boat with Rethink many years later!

My Side Hustle: Real Estate

In 2009, nine years into my work at Integrity, I asked someone for directions on an airport train and wound up moving to Denver about 10 months later to get married to him.

Keeping one household is cheaper than two. With the budget we freed up, we decided to buy a ski condo in the mountains, which we rented out on VRBO (Vacation Rental by Owner).

I didn't know the ski rental market, so I found the prospect mildly terrifying. Would anyone rent? Or would I just be on the hook for an extra mortgage now?

But Ned was a skier and knew his audience. It was his idea to buy a slope-side, one-bedroom place in a building full of studios and then to update the 1980s décor.

"In the winter, everything books, so it doesn't matter," he said. "But in the summer, when people have more choice, they'll want the nicer unit with the extra room."

He was right.

A few years later, he noticed an uptick in construction in the once-sleepy downtown Denver area around Union Station.

At the time, the economy was still coming back from the global financial crisis. Real estate prices and interest rates were low. And yet VRBO was becoming just as popular in cities as it was in the mountains. So anyone who could afford a down payment and furnishings could then rent out a space for hotel prices.

We bought one condo and discovered the rents we brought in could more than cover the mortgage. "Why isn't everyone doing this?" Ned asked. We bought another, and a third, renting to business travelers, grandparents coming to see grandkids, doctors in town for conferences.

Five years later, every time we took a seat at a Denver bar to eat tacos, the people around us would be talking about buying investment real estate. By then, prices had risen and Denver had imposed a 30-day rental minimum. Real estate was still a good investment. It just wasn't an insanely good investment anymore.

This was a lesson to me that market opportunities can be visible a long time before people take action on them – and that the right time to take action is often when they still feel risky. In business, you want to get ahead of the crowd.

Founding Rethink Compliance

By 2015, Integrity had been bought by SAI Global and combined with a few other compliance learning businesses. The other early players had gotten big, too.

Meanwhile, I was restless. Every day, clients were asking for more innovation – for courses that looked more like the iPhones and sleek websites of that time's digital media. But the big, mature companies didn't seem to be equipped to deliver something truly new.

I had never contemplated starting my own business. And yet, it was so clear to me where the market needed to go – and no one else was moving that way. I found I wanted full creative and business control. I had strong opinions about how a next-generation compliance business should be structured and run. I wanted to call the shots and see if I was right.

To me, that left only one choice: to resign from my job. I opened Rethink's doors on July 1, 2015, initially taking on only code of conduct work. My first team consisted of a lawyer and a graphic designer, both part-time, both home with kids, both deeply talented.

Of course, I had no idea of the journey that lay ahead. I didn't yet know how much I would need to stretch myself or how thrilling it all would be. That said, I wish I'd had a book like this to give me a glimpse of what was ahead – I might have gotten to some of my best ideas faster!

Trial and Error

So much of being an entrepreneur is trying things out and learning through trial and error.

When you're the founder, you do everything from identifying market opportunities to interviewing accountants to picking out the company's check designs. Basically, anything that is not explicitly someone else's job is your job, especially in the early days.

In the book that follows, we'll talk about key entrepreneurial topics – like identifying good market opportunities, putting your infrastructure in place, handling your finances, and building out your team, if you want one.

You Don't Need to Know Everything to Start

People sometimes look at our journeys and say, "Wow, what a leap!" But, in reality, there was very little leaping involved. As you'll see in the pages ahead, a lot happened in slow, careful steps. We learned what we needed to know as we went along.

Initially, all of us really only had one plan: make more money than we spent. We didn't yet know what shape the companies would take, which clients we would serve, or even where the business would come from. But we knew what the market wanted and believed we could figure out the rest.

Get Ready to Be Humbled

"Leading a business is some of the most fun I've ever had. It has also been, in every way, an awesome challenge," said Kirsten. As a leader, you will get a chance to see your strengths in action, and you will also come face to face with your own limitations.

One of the best characteristics you can bring to the job is the humility to know when you are not the right person for a specific job or task – or when you need to grow yourself so you can be the right person. Kirsten reflected, "Over the years, some of my best decisions have come when I 'fired' myself from a role so I could hire or promote someone better."

Go All-In

Some people choose to dip a toe in the water, but our advice is to go all-in, at least emotionally. If you choose to take the entrepreneurial plunge, it will be easier to stay committed if you start committed. The journey is too difficult for people who allow themselves to easily waver.

"I just wanted to make it for at least six months so it didn't look like I was fired," joked Kristy. "Going all-in meant that if I were to fail, I'd do so knowing I gave it my absolute all. I think people avoid committing to try their hardest so they can give themselves an excuse – 'I didn't really try that hard, and I'm sure I could have succeeded if I had.' That wasn't for me."

Committing to the entrepreneurship path makes the road easier. And as we all know, the journey of a thousand miles begins with the first step. Are you ready for your first step? Of course you are. Let's begin!

SECTION ONE
Pre-Launch

In this section, we'll go into what you need to do to start your business, from the time you're in-house all the way to launch day. You'll learn what you can (and can't) do to prepare while you're still in your job, then we'll go into deciding what your company will do and how you'll do it. We'll discuss structures for your business and how to choose one that will work for you. Lastly, we'll go into the challenges of financing and obtaining capital and discuss your options to fund your dream.

CHAPTER 2

While You are Still In-house

W hile you are still in-house, you want to start thinking about how to make the jump and how to have a successful business. It is certainly wise to be prepared for your next step. Most people decide to start their business while still at their current job.

For months before taking the plunge, Kristy spent each lunch hour Googling things like "how to have a successful consulting business" and "getting clients for consulting." Reading articles is important, but there are other things you should do while still in-house that can make a big difference for your successful transition.

In this book we do not provide legal advice, so please consult with legal counsel who is familiar with employment issues. There are, nevertheless, points we can raise here for your consideration.

Be Fair to Your Employer

When you are first thinking about leaving, there is likely no reason to discuss this with the company or your boss. After all, you may ultimately decide to stay, and telling people you were thinking of leaving may not be a good career move. But, when you are further along, you should be thinking about what is fair to all concerned.

Once you've decided to quit, it is best to tell your employer that you are starting a business. One reason for doing this should be obvious: It is the nature of the field. It is called compliance and ethics. Being ethical is especially important. If the industry identifies you as someone who cheats, this can look very bad. If you are going to make a living from telling companies how to be ethical, you have to be a role model.

Many people choose to fess up when they formally resign; but if you feel able to say something sooner, you may find that people at your current job can assist you with moral support or referrals, even before you leave.

Notice Periods

Consider how long your notice period is likely to be. For many Americans, this may be as little as two weeks. In some companies, as soon as you resign, you are marched out of the building so as not to be a security risk. In the UK, Europe, and much of the rest of the world, your employment contract will dictate the terms of your leaving.

Kristy's contract as chief compliance officer in the UK had an exceptionally long notice period of six months. She faithfully served every last day. This period was tremendously useful, as she was able to tell the company that she was leaving to start her own firm, and was therefore not hiding her intentions. It also gave her a long runway to use to prepare for her launch.

Preparing to Start Before You Start

How much can you do to get started while you are still in-house? This depends on your relationship with your employer and your boss. Some companies will not want you earning any money in the field prior to your departure. Others may be more comfortable with it. If you're going to start working or making money in your business before you leave your current role, you may need to disclose this.

Before Joe even thought of leaving his employment, he was being offered payment for advice and presentations in the then-nascent compliance and ethics field. He made sure that his boss knew what he was doing and where he was going for speaking engagements. Joe set up a separate personal bank account in which to keep his speaking fees. He used this money exclusively for compliance-related materials and to travel to speak at compliance conferences if he believed the travel couldn't be justified as benefitting the company. Joe's employer benefited from Joe's exposure to new information, and Joe's reputation in the field enhanced the employer's reputation as a compliance leader.

Joe was able write and research extensively on his own time. Back then, research meant spending lunchtimes in libraries reading journals and books. Often the results of the work could also be used to benefit his employer.

Financial Preparation

Preparation also includes getting your finances in order. So, from the beginning, look for ways to strengthen your financial position.

Where there is a company savings plan, or any system for putting money aside, utilize it to the max. The more you can reduce debt and build a reserve, the better it is for your business start-up phase.

> The more you can reduce debt and build a reserve, the better it is for your business start-up phase.

You can also take other steps, such as getting a financial advisor, an accountant, and a lawyer. None of that interferes with your work for your current employer as long as you do it on your own time. There is a detailed section on preparing financially and obtaining capital later in this book.

Utilizing In-House Resources

Can you use your company administrative staff, copy machine, and office materials? The temptation is very strong. It is so easy, and it can seem easy to hide. But even though it may seem small to you, it is on the wrong side of the line. Part of your preparation for how you are going to run your new business is considering how you are going to do these little but important things.

It is better to find ways to do these on your own dime and your own time. Remember, too, that if you are at all successful in your new business, you will have employees. They will know your story. If you "stole" from your past employer – even in little ways – guess what message that sends to your own employees?

Leave on Good Terms

When you've decided to start your own business, it can be easy to slack off to focus on your new enterprise at work. Don't do it. Leaving on good terms is critical for your long-term reputation. You should continue to work diligently until your time with your employer is complete. You are being paid for your time and energy, and the employer should be getting what it is paying for.

There is a maxim in consulting that your previous employer is frequently your first client. There is a good reason for this. First, you already know the ins and outs of the company from which you came. Second, you're probably now less expensive to your current company in the aggregate, since the company is no longer paying your payroll taxes or for your benefits. If feasible, try to negotiate a contract with your employer for a set number of hours or a project once you've left. If you can do this, you will be in a much better cash flow position when the business officially launches.

Navigating Non-Compete and Non-Solicitation Agreements

Go back into your files or email to see if you signed a non-compete agreement. In many parts of the world, it is standard practice for employees to sign agreements promising not to compete with their former employer for a set number of months. If you have signed such an agreement, review the terms carefully. You don't want to be dealing with a lawsuit when you've just started your business.

Kirsten navigated a complex situation when she left her former employer and started a business in the same field. She had signed a non-compete when she joined the company, which remained in force for one year after leaving. So she sought legal advice to understand what she was and was not permitted to do under its terms.

That said, she also got very lucky: The year before she left, her employer decided to exit a line of business in which she specialized. When she left, she had copies of all-company emails from the head of client services and the CFO announcing they were no longer offering this particular service. So she started her business offering exactly this solution – since there could be no argument that she was violating her non-compete.

To complicate things further, her former employer also became one of her first clients, hiring Rethink for a variety of projects, including writing courses for clients and the library. To take on this work, she negotiated a new non-compete, one that was fair to both sides, and honored it fully. When former colleagues raised concerns about her possible conflicts of interest as a business owner, she referred them to the agreement.

Not everyone will want this kind of complexity. But there are ways to navigate it and honor your commitments while still being an advocate for your own best interests.

In addition to non-compete agreements, review your contract to see if you signed a non-solicitation agreement. A non-solicitation agreement stipulates that you are unable to hire away employees at your current company for several months after you leave. It's best to know whether you are under such obligations before luring away top talent at your current employer. When it comes to such contracts, however, don't wing it or try to be your own lawyer; get competent legal advice.

Intellectual Property Ownership

Who owns the work you created while you were in-house? This not an area for guesswork or just going by your instincts or what you think you can get away with. Where there are any written or graphic materials involved, any patentable ideas, or any business, product, or service names involved, do not guess. Talk with a lawyer who knows this field. You may be fortunate and have an employer who is happy to share this material. But they are not obligated to do so. You may have written an excellent FCPA compliance policy for the company, but the company owns that.

In many cases, the things you create as part of your employment may be owned by your employer. There are essentially four types of intellectual property protection: 1) patents; 2) trade and service marks; 3) copyright; and 4) trade secrets. If you want to use anything from your prior employer, get sound advice.

Of course, your employer can give you permission; although even this can be a bit tricky. If your immediate boss says, "sure, go ahead and use that document, or idea, or logo," you want to be sure that will hold up. This is not to say that every idea you have or everything you write while an employee belongs to your employer. But it does mean you have to be alert on these points and get appropriate legal advice. Even a topic that might seem simple, like having company materials on your personal laptop, can require some thought.

Of course, to the extent it is true, you can certainly tell others about your work for the company as long as it was not confidential or otherwise restricted. If you drafted the code of conduct and it is posted online, you can certainly tell people that and refer them to it. But if a client of your new company hires you to write a code for them, do not mistakenly think you own your prior employer's code. Here, there is no substitute for getting solid legal advice.

What You Should Do Now

It is likely that in your new company your experience will be a key asset. So, while you are in-house, learn as much about the field as possible. Participate in compliance functions whenever and wherever you can. Talk with and learn from your in-house experts. Take your internal auditor to lunch and start to learn that area. Your company benefits from your depth of knowledge, and you are building a personal asset – your experience – that will be valuable in your future business.

Once you've crossed your 't's and dotted your 'i's, it's time to begin planning in earnest. It's one thing to dream about starting a business; it's a whole other thing to launch one.

Later in the book, we will go into details about writing, public speaking, and networking. These are important for both your pre- and post-launch and should be a focus before leaving your job. But for now, look through your contract or employment manual and prepare to leave on good terms, then prepare your answer to the question you'll be asked hundreds of times: what does your company do?

CHAPTER 3

Who are You and what do You Do?

There is an art to the "elevator pitch." An elevator pitch is a 30-second statement about your company and what it does. It should be deliverable in the time it takes to ride an elevator up several floors with a potential prospect.

While an elevator pitch sounds easy, creating it requires making a tremendous number of decisions. For instance, what is your company's name? What does it specialize in? What about your products or services differentiates them from the crowd? In this chapter, we'll go into those critical questions so that you can craft your pitch successfully.

What's in a Name?

Shakespeare famously wrote, "What's in a name? That which we call a rose by any other name would smell as sweet." While intrinsic properties may be enough to propel floral popularity, in business, your notoriety and memorability will be driven first by your business' name.

Choosing a name is more art than science, and also a topic about which you can lose an afternoon to Google research. It is worth doing some deep thinking up front because, of all the decisions you will make, this is among the hardest to change.

For example:

- Any legal structure you set up (as we cover later in this section) will be tied to that name.
- Any agreements you make, from leases to client contracts, will be tied to your company name and tax ID.
- Any brochures or other printed company materials will bear that name.

Also, from the first day you start doing business, you will build a reputation and goodwill associated with your company's name, some of which can be lost or diluted if the name changes.

So take the time and care upfront to select a name that will serve you for a while.

Our Experiences

"When we started Integrity Interactive, we wanted a name that connected with what we were providing," Joe said. "'Integrity' moved us away from the ongoing debate between 'ethics' and 'compliance' and indicated that we included a values orientation. 'Interactive' suggested technology, but also a fundamental point in compliance: Any compliance message cannot be just one-way communications. There needs to be active involvement by the employees. So the name and the product design reflected this thinking."

Finding the name for Kristy's company was hard work. She wanted something that reflected her energy and sensibility about compliance. One Saturday night she stayed up until 4 a.m. working with a friend to create a shortlist of possible names. "We came up with variations on energy themes – fire, ignition, light, kindle. We got down to a shortlist and then Googled all of the terms on the shortlist, along with the terms 'compliance' and 'consulting,' to find out if the names were taken. In the end, Spark Compliance Consulting was the best choice, and the company was born."

Kirsten chose the name Rethink Compliance during a long "think" session on a plane home from London. "I wanted our name to immediately register as different from the companies we were positioning against," Kirsten said. "I also wanted to reflect a concept I had heard from so many clients – namely, that the standards for compliance content and materials had changed and we needed to move on from old approaches and methods. The name "Rethink" is our way of saying, 'Let's step back and think about the best way to do this.'"

Consider Spelling Out What You Do

When naming your company, consider spelling out what you do. "One of the reasons we chose 'Spark Compliance Consulting' was so that anyone Googling 'compliance consulting' would likely come up with us." By using the word 'consulting,' people immediately knew what Spark Compliance did without going to the website. If your company specializes in training, consider using the word "training" in your name. Not only will your specialization be obvious to anyone reading the company's name, but Google will also be more likely to display your website because your site will be full of the keywords people are looking for.

If you're not planning on having a true specialty, or if you think you may branch out into several types of services or products over time, you may want to keep your company's name more general.

Will It Sell in the End?

We go into detail about selling your company in chapter 15. However, it's worth mentioning here that, in naming your company, you should consider how the name may affect your ability to sell the company in the future.

"I deliberately chose not to name my company Kristy Grant-Hart Consulting or Kristy Grant-Hart and Associates," said Kristy. She wanted to be sure that if Spark Compliance were eventually acquired, it wouldn't always have to be associated with her. "A buyer might want to integrate Spark

Compliance into their company, or they might want it to be a standalone brand without my involvement."

Another reason not to name the company after yourself is that doing so can make your company seem small or brand you as a solo enterprise, even if you bring on associates or partners.

Despite these considerations, there are reasons for naming your business after yourself. If you have developed a name and reputation in the industry, it will make it easier to find you if your name is on the business.

So, What Do You Do?

One of the most fundamental (and potentially most consequential decisions) as a founder is this: What does my company do? Everything else about your company will flow from this one decision, including:

- who you hire or team up with
- how you market and sell
- how much upfront capital you need
- what your cash flow looks like
- where you look for business
- who your competitors are
- how you grow and how fast you grow

Taking the time upfront to make a clear and strategic decision can make the difference between a business that muddles along and a business that takes off – though, as we'll talk about at the end of this chapter, you can always adjust and improve your decision if you need to.

Where Is the Need?

In a fascinating article in Forbes by Neil Patel called "90% of Start-Ups Fail: Here's What To Know About The Other 10%," Patel reports on a truth about start-up life that should be blindingly obvious — but can be easy to overlook when you're caught up in the excitement of getting a business off the ground:

One major reason start-ups fail is if they offer something no one wants.

He cites one well-regarded survey of failed start-ups. The top reason, selected by 42% of those interviewed: "A lack of market need."

It's worth mentioning that the second reason, "ran out of cash," is also directly related to the first problem. As Patel points out, one great way to avoid running out of cash is to sell more and grow fast.

But this makes sense. We've seen it in our own lives! There's the trendy shop that pops up downtown, maybe with expensive interior design and good press coverage. It opens to great hoopla (though you never go, or only go once), languishes for a bit, loses steam, and eventually closes its doors – an expensive lesson in product-market fit for its owners and investors.

What was the problem? Not enough people wanted what they were selling: neither the way they were offering it, nor at the price point they were selling it. The owners loved the idea, but the market demand just wasn't there.

As Patel writes, "If you're going to spend your time making a product, then spend your time making sure it's the right product for the right market."

This means that, when you begin to answer the question "what does my company do?" don't start inside your own head.

The Right and Wrong Questions

Don't ponder what you're passionate about or only take inventory of your own skills and interests. There will be time to match your talents to the business. Getting the right fit comes first.

Instead, look outward and approach the question with humility, knowing that many smart and well-intentioned people don't get this right and commit themselves to a business or product plan too early before they've really proved it works.

Take a close look at your market and the people you'll be selling to. Ask yourself the following:

- What are companies/people in the marketplace buying today?
- What do they need?
- Where are the gaps?
- Where are the pain points?
- Where are market needs not being met, or not being met as well as they could be?
- What do practitioners complain about when they talk about vendors or consultants?
- Where do they feel they lack options?
- What new products or services do they need – and have money to pay for – that are not being supplied, or not being supplied in the way they want?

Keep in mind it's a hundred times easier to sell someone something they are already planning to buy than it is to talk them into buying something they've never thought about. You can always expand into new markets later, after you've found success with existing ones.

When Joe and his colleagues started Integrity Interactive, they were offering a product everyone needed – compliance training. Customers knew they should be doing it but were stymied because they couldn't deliver training on a mass scale without a massive in-person travel budget for the compliance team.

By offering online training, Integrity Interactive was giving clients the ability to reach employees on a scale never before possible, at a price that was a fraction of what live training would have cost if it had even been feasible on such a large scale. Pricing reflected not the incremental cost of training (which for online training was small) but the value to the customers. Customers who already knew they needed training now had a cheaper, more flexible way to meet their needs.

As a compliance professional, you may have developed ways to read your company's employees, collect information and insights about culture, and understand attitudes that you used to shape your program. Turn those same skills to your new audience, the compliance buyer.

Look at what the market is asking for. Listen for the comments, complaints, and questions that come up again and again. Then ask yourself what the market needs that you know you can deliver. That's where your business idea should start.

Specialize for Better Results

Here, we are going to encourage you to do something that many new business creators tend to resist: specialize. By which we mean focus on providing a particular product/service or serving a particular subset of the market.

For most founders, this will feel counterintuitive. After all, when you start a business, you want business from anyone who will give it to you! When your biggest challenge is getting paying clients, it can feel downright risky to pre-emptively rule out any opportunities.

Specializing takes courage. It means narrowing your options. But put yourself in your clients' shoes for a minute.

Let's say that, as the founder of a new business, you are looking for a bookkeeper and accountant. Is the best accountant for you someone who works with anyone? Whose client list runs the gamut, from small mom-and-pop shops to fast-growing SaaS technology start-ups to Fortune 10 companies? Or would you rather work with an accountant that specializes in businesses just like yours, who knows what you are likely to need and the issues you may face? Kirsten, who went through five different bookkeeping and accounting services before she found the right match, would suggest the latter!

Companies that will do anything for anyone are special to no one. They don't stand out. Companies that do a particular thing or serve a particular type of client can set themselves apart.

Think, for example, of what a client's online search will look like. Will they search for just anyone who does training, or will they search for training in the risk area they need to address, such as FCPA? Clients will usually focus specifically on what they need. The more your business matches that need, the more likely they are to connect with you. With success and time, the ones that specialize can become known for what they do. It's the marketing and sales version of compound interest.

Joe had worked for 20 years in telecommunications, antitrust, and later FCPA. It was obvious that those would be areas of focus for him professionally. But when Joe was starting in business, the entire field of compliance and ethics was new. So at that time, in 1996, when the number of players was much smaller, the field of compliance and ethics was, to an extent, enough of a specialty. Even so, he made it clear that he addressed organizational compliance and ethics, and he was not a professional business ethicist. He did not purport to be an expert on right and wrong, but only on organizational conduct.

In contrast, by the time Kristy started Spark Compliance in 2015, corporate compliance and ethics was too broad a category to stand out. She quickly realized that she was getting swamped in a sea of other consultants all offering consulting in compliance. Kristy shifted to focus on the idea of being a translator from the US to the UK/Europe in the compliance profession. Because she's an American who had been living in the UK for several years, she'd developed the talent of being able to explain the UK/European laws in a way Americans would understand, and vice versa. This enabled her to quickly sign very large enterprises, which became the core of Spark Compliance's business.

Kirsten knew what she wanted to do from day one. She had built up valuable experience in online training and the compliance field at Integrity Interactive, plus had a background in journalism with its focus on clear communications. So when she launched Rethink, she focused the business on creating great compliance content, specifically how clients could use modern, digitally-savvy communications to get and keep their employees' attention.

Take the "Four Corners Approach" to Specialization

How do you decide where and how to focus? One way to do this is to consider focusing on four elements of compliance and ethics, which we call the "Four Corner Approach." The corners are:

- Compliance function (e.g., training, helplines, investigations, etc.);
- Compliance risk area (e.g., privacy, FCPA/corruption, antitrust, environment);
- Geographic area (e.g., Delaware Valley, northeast US, national and regional such as the EU, global); and
- Industry (e.g., healthcare, financial services, high tech)

You could choose just one, or a combination. For instance, you could be a training expert willing to work anywhere in any industry dealing with any risk. Or you could focus on antitrust training in the US in the technology industry.

Corner One: Compliance Function

What practice area has the most appeal to you, is your strongest area, and represents a good market? It can be useful to start with an inventory of functions. The list here does not purport to be absolute. It draws from the basics of the Sentencing Guidelines standards. It may inspire you to develop one of these areas or develop an entirely different one.

- Codes of conduct and policies
- Practices and internal controls
- Background checks on hires and promotions
- Due diligence on third parties
- Monitoring of third parties
- Compliance auditing
- Compliance monitoring

- Compliance monitoring using data analytics
- Program evaluations
- Reporting systems
- Prevention of retaliation
- Training
- Communications
- Incentives
- Discipline
- Investigations
- Risk assessment

Look at this list to determine your interests and strengths. If you have conducted investigations and like this type of activity, consider moving in that direction. If you have dealt with reporting systems, but see a gap that needs to be filled, you might think about developing a service to close that gap.

Corner Two: Compliance Risk Area

Corner two focuses on specific areas of compliance risk. Specific risk relates to challenges created by one law or a series of laws on one subject or subject area.

Some options include:

- Accounting fraud
- Antitrust
- FCPA/corruption
- Privacy
- Money laundering
- Environmental compliance
- Product safety
- Export controls
- Human slavery
- Insider trading

- Conflicts of interest
- Discrimination
- Harassment
- Immigration
- Consumer protection
- Government contracting
- Intellectual property infringement
- Political contributions/lobbying
- Regulated industries
- Wage and hour/FLSA
- Workplace safety

Selecting a risk area or risks is just like choosing any area of focus. Ask yourself: What is your relevant experience? What do you know about each area? What value can you add? What are others not covering adequately? What do you see happening in that market? What enforcement initiatives have not gotten widespread attention? For example, if privacy is your focus, you might view the evolving laws in the EU and California and recognize that their expansion is inevitable in your part of the world, or in a particular industry. You might then start to build your credentials in that area, including writing and setting the groundwork for public speaking.

Corner Three: Geographic Area

Corner three revolves around geographic area. In this context, geography can mean the area in which you work or the area in which you have your specialty. For example, someone with a specialty in the European General Data Protection Regulation might consider their geography "Europe," even if they live in the US.

Geography might also relate to the area in which you live. There are many service providers and consultants that live in London and practice exclusively within the city.

One might assume that, compared to compliance function and risk area, geography would be relatively straightforward. But you need to consider your quality of life and how much you are willing to travel for work. Do you want to be spending much of your life on the road? While some compliance work may be done remotely, other work requires onsite visits. Being the global expert on developments in a key risk area, such as privacy, may call on you to be on the road frequently. Doing live training or conducting investigations can also lead to extensive travel.

Be sure to think about your lifestyle before committing to a geography. Do you want to be home with your children every night, or are you happy freewheeling to dinners in new countries every day? Can your partner/spouse travel with you sometimes so you can see new places together when you're done with your work? Are day trips fine with you, but two-week onsite investigations too much? These considerations are important.

Travel can be fantastic, but it can also take its toll. Each of us has seen talented consultants burn out from the travel required of them.

Language is also an important factor. If you want to cover Latin America, it helps to speak other languages, particularly Spanish and Brazilian Portuguese. If your work is doing live training, working in an area where you do not effectively speak the language is an obvious disadvantage.

You should not, however, simply assume that your market has to be your own country. Joe has studied several languages but speaks only one. However, he has traveled the world in the compliance and ethics field and worked with companies, NGOs and governments without a problem. Similarly, Kirsten's company serves many multinationals, including companies headquartered throughout the world.

It is also worth considering that, while your particular geographic area may be saturated in the risk area that interests you most, there may still be an enormous opportunity in other markets. India represents an enormous opportunity for the development of the compliance field. Another example is Colombia, where the enactment of a law to address corruption has expanded business opportunities in compliance.

For those with a desire to work internationally in this field, there is certainly great opportunity. But it is also helpful to remember that there is no such place as "international." Each country has its unique characteristics, and each is worth studying if you intend to do anything there.

Corner Four: Industry

The fourth corner is industry. Industry can relate to a specific type of work, like manufacturing or oil and gas. Industry can also refer to sub-groups, like non-profit groups, colleges/universities, or associations. Wherever people work in groups within organizations, there is a need for compliance.

A large proportion of people in the field work in generalized corporate compliance. "Corporate compliance" tends to mean companies outside the very highly-regulated industries like health care, financial services, universities/colleges, insurance, and the like. You may also observe a phenomenon in these highly-regulated industries where those involved believe they are unique and unlike anyone else in the world. This can cause them only to listen to those who have been in their industry and close their doors to others whom they consider outsiders. If you want to work in these environments, it is probably best to specialize.

When selecting an industry, it may make sense to start by considering those that relate to your background. You can then look for similarities or common touch points with other industries. For instance, if someone has experience in the regulated telecommunications industry, the practitioner could tout her experience dealing with the regulatory environment when speaking with potential clients in other regulated industries.

When assessing an industry, remember to consider macroeconomic trends. For example, someone specializing in the coal industry would need to consider the likely replacement of that fuel source. Someone looking at transportation would need to consider how environmental factors might shift the fortunes of that industry.

Putting It Together

Now that you've read through all four of the considerations, choose what works for you. Ultimately you will do your best work when:

- The specialty, risk area, or industry you choose is interesting to you.
- You naturally read or write about the area you choose.
- The lifestyle that comes with your choice is compatible with the life you want.
- You can imagine yourself doing the same work in five years and it makes you smile.

Specializing can be a powerful driver of sales and marketing. When you do one thing well, people come to you for that one thing. When you do everything, no one thinks of you first. Once you are firmly established, you can always broaden your focus, but your business should make sense and not be an unconnected grab bag of offerings.

One last thing – remember that you can always pivot. Most companies are founded with one set of expectations, then pivot to something more lucrative once they've tested the market with their original idea. After all, YouTube was started as a video-based dating site. If they can pivot that much, so can your business.

CHAPTER 4

Choosing Your Business Model

The world of business can be broken into models. Take home mainte-nance for instance. In one model, the roofer comes and replaces the roof, then has to continually look for customers whose homes need re-roofing. In the second model, the person with a lawnmower signs a con-tract to mow the lawn twice a month for a year. In the third, the owner of the lawnmowing company signs several contracts to mow lawns twice a month, then hires people to mow the lawns, paying them an hourly rate to do so while keeping the profit. Which model is best for you? That depends entirely on your goals and resources.

Products vs. Services

One of the first decisions you'll make is whether you sell products or ser-vices. A "product" is defined as "an article or substance that is manufac-tured or refined for sale." "Service" is defined as "the act of helping or doing work for someone."

The lines between products and services can be blurry in the compliance profession. Is the delivery of an anti-bribery policy a product or service? On one hand, it's a physical thing that can be printed. On the other hand, poli-cies are frequently provided by consultants charging an hourly rate for their time.

There are pros and cons to selling either. The model you choose will be based on several factors. These include: (1) which model you prefer that fits your business objectives; (2) which model lends itself to your specific expertise; (3) which model the market tells you it wants from you; and (4) which model is supported by the resources you have available to you in terms of capital, time, technology, and staff. Let's take a deeper look at the differences between products and services.

The Service of Consulting

Many people dream of going out on their own, serving only the clients they choose to work with, jumping in to save the day, and offering sage advice that improves the business. Most consultants start off as individuals operating on their own. These people are frequently referred to as "solos."

Solo consulting comes with many benefits. The first is control over your time. You are not beholden to a partner or firm. You can choose your clients (at least in theory), and you can choose the projects you prefer.

Being solo means that you can often price yourself at more competitive rates than larger firms. Solos usually have home-based offices, so they don't tend to have high overhead like larger firms that need more hourly revenue to make the same amount of profit.

Many solos love the consistency of stepping in for a person on a long maternity leave, performing a multi-month audit, or completing a discreet in-house/in-office project. The money made during such opportunities can fund time off later and can enable financial planning for the next several months or year(s).

Three months after Spark Compliance was launched, Kristy took an assignment as an interim CCO for a company for which she'd previously worked. She was working as a consultant but was effectively in-house-as she was in the office several days a week managing the day-to-day compliance program. Since she knew the people and how the company operated, it was a natural fit.

While she was deeply grateful for the steady work and consistent client payments, she found herself in a quandary. Because she was working full time for one client, she found it enormously difficult to take sales meetings or sales calls to try to find more work; even if she was able to take on other projects, it would have been nearly impossible to find time to do them. She felt that she had all the responsibilities of a CCO without the perks of retirement contributions and sick days. It wasn't for her.

Once Kristy completed that client's project, she chose to reject in-house-type assignments in favor of multiple projects for multiple clients at one time, such as risk assessments and program reviews, neither of which required her to be in her client's offices. "There was risk in that decision, as it stopped the steady paycheck. But I realized that if I wanted a steady paycheck, I would have stayed in-house. For me, the jump from quasi-in-house to out-of-office consultant was the right one."

Productizing Your Service – Whether Solo or Not

For many compliance practitioners, the dream of consulting is working with many companies at one time, like external legal counsel tends to do. If you're trying to get this type of work, it helps to productize your services. What does this mean? It means presenting your services as projects that have a beginning, a middle, and an end, and positioning those products as services that you perform frequently for many different clients.

Kristy learned how to do this during her "mastermind" with Kirsten. The concept of a mastermind comes from Napoleon Hill's famous book, *Think and Grow Rich*. In it, Hill exhorts his audience to find one to four like-minded people with whom to meet every one to two weeks. In these meetings, the participants share their wins and losses. They also help each other to work through professional challenges, and to hold each other accountable for the goals set for their business.

During one of Kirsten and Kristy's mastermind sessions, Kirsten explained the idea of productizing consulting work. This involved changing Kristy's offerings from sharing compliance-related knowledge to specific, concrete products. Kristy changed the wording on the Spark Compliance website, as well as her ideas about what she offered. She changed:

From	To
Risk review and management	Risk Assessments
GDPR and privacy-related services	GDPR Audits
Compliance program optimization	Compliance Program Review
Compliance program assistance	Compliance Program Gap Analysis and Recommendations Report

The change in wording signalled to the world that Spark's services were compact. Many clients continued to hire Spark Compliance to give ongoing advice and to perform work on an ad hoc basis. However, the changes on the Spark website indicated that acting full-time as an in-house CCO wasn't one of the products offered.

Productizing your services is easier if there is more than one consultant at your firm. Many clients want more than a "single point of failure." If a solo gets sick, overwhelmed, or has an emergency, there will be no one else able to deliver the work. Having more than one consultant at the firm who can handle workflow can make clients feel secure. Also, having overflow capacity if you get too busy can be useful, especially if two large reports are due at the same time. Plus, if one person is busy, the other has time to work on sales and marketing.

Recurring Revenue Challenges

Regardless of whether you're a solo or not, one of the challenges of consulting is that it lends itself to one-off projects. That is, it follows the roofer model described earlier. As soon as one client's project is done, you're back onto the hamster wheel of trying to win new business. You may also realize that it is just when you are busiest, doing a major project for one client, that you need to be marketing to be sure there is work after the current project is done.

Do clients come back again and again? Absolutely, especially if you've done a good job the first time. But clients will only carry out major projects like risk assessments or program reviews every two to three years. There is a constant need to develop new business or to try to reengage past clients, which many consultants find disheartening and exhausting.

Some consultants are able to bring in consistent cash flow using a retainer model. In a retainer model, the client agrees to purchase a certain number of hours per month, usually at a discounted hourly rate. If they don't use all of their hours one month, the hours roll over into the next month. Retainer models are great, but many clients don't want to commit to a large annual number. Regardless, it's worth trying to move clients to this model, as having control over cash flow is a vital part of your business, and retainer clients give a strong base from which to grow.

Compliance Products

Many companies offer products to compliance professionals. These include eLearning courses, books, due diligence reports, and software for everything from risk management to sanctions screening. Every year the number of vendors serving the compliance profession gets larger. But that doesn't mean that your idea can't stand out.

Pricing Model

As discussed previously, one of the major challenges with service-based consulting is that it is typically purchased in one-off transactions. Many products in the compliance space are also sold this way. For example, books and due diligence reports are typically one-time purchases.

The alternative to this model is to offer subscription-based product delivery with multi-year contracts. Examples include eLearning courses, due diligence storage platforms, sanctions review products with continual monitoring, whistle-blower hotline services, and communications libraries. Companies offering these types of products tend to require one- to three-year contracts, with multi-year contracts attracting better prices and greater incentives.

Why wouldn't everyone build a product with a recurring revenue model? Many of these products require a great deal of capital to start. Developing a go-to-market library of online courses (and their translations, if you plan to serve global companies) can take months, if not years, and require both a team and a large capital investment upfront. Most companies trying to self-fund are unlikely to be in a position to afford this.

Iteration

Many solos and companies transition from one type of service or product to another over time. Kristy started out briefly as a solo, then added a partner, then employees to her service-based consulting work. As we saw in the introduction, at the same time, she was publishing books and online training courses for compliance officers, which are products.

Most companies evolve their offering over time. Starting as a solo consultant takes the smallest amount of capital and is the fastest business to start. Creating a subscription-based product is usually the most capital-intensive and time-consuming way of starting a business, but it offers the greatest opportunity for aggressive growth.

At the end of the day, there isn't a silver bullet. Whether you choose to be a roofer, a lawnmower, or a person managing a lawnmowing company, whatever works best for you right now is the place you should start.

CHAPTER 5

Building Your Company's Infrastructure

P eople use the phrase "starting a business" as if it is a single moment in time. But starting a business requires many steps – some internal, like deciding what your business will do; and some external, like filing the paperwork to start your company from a legal point of view.

Company Structure

Early on, you will need to decide on your company's legal structure – some version of incorporation that will let you do business as an entity rather than an individual. To protect yourself, it's critical that you put this legal structure in place sooner rather than later.

On these points, as with tax questions, it is essential that you get professional legal advice. We offer our perspectives here based on our experiences, but it is not legal advice; your lawyer must do that for you.

Once you've legally established a business, this entity can sign contracts, take out loans or credit, and face legal liability without putting your personal assets, savings, or credit report at risk. However, you may quickly find that some of those you deal with, such as banks, will not rely on your business entity and will require you to sign as a guarantor so that you are also responsible for any debts.

Keep in mind that your risk increases as you launch products, serve clients or users, and add employees, so get this done early.

For simple company structures, registration can be done online. Kirsten set up her DBA ("doing business as" or business name) and initial single-owner LLC using LegalZoom. Then, as the business got more complex, she hired outside lawyers for future company iterations.

Which Structure to Pick?

Deciding on a company structure can feel daunting. After all, this one choice will affect:

- how much you pay in taxes
- your ability to raise money
- the paperwork you need to file
- your personal liability

When you start a business, much about the future can seem murky so it can feel hard to decide.

Something worth bearing in mind is that it's typically easier to move from a simpler company structure to a more complex type than it is to go the other way.

If you genuinely feel stuck, one strategy could be to pick the simplest company structure you need for your purposes now and reserve the option to change this in the future. "Rethink Compliance has changed its company structure three times as our needs and footprint changed," Kirsten said.

Your Options

The following section is United States-specific; however, most countries have some variation of these business types in place. For non-US entrepreneurs, check with a local lawyer to find the best business structure for your enterprise.

In the US, your options include:

Sole proprietorship

This is the simplest kind of business entity. If you want to operate under a different company name, you simply file a DBA form, which is easy to find online. Keep in mind, however, that the choice of name can be complicated if someone else already has rights to that name. (This, again, is an area where legal counsel is important.)

Once your DBA is in place, you can open up a bank account and receive checks in the company's name.

Sole proprietorships are inexpensive to set up and easy to dissolve. Taxes are straightforward, as any business income is simply reported on your personal income taxes (although all of these matters are covered by state and sometimes local laws). However, as a significant downside, there is no legal separation between you and the business, so this structure offers very little personal protection from risk. Instead, the business is seen as an extension of you.

Limited liability corporation (LLC)

This is a good first step for anyone with the ambition to build a serious, ongoing business. Like all the possible business structures, in the US this is a matter of state law, and you would need legal advice in each circumstance.

An LLC legal structure limits the personal liability and risk exposure for owners, partners, and equity holders because of actions taken by the company. Unless you have otherwise provided a personal guarantee, owners aren't responsible for company debt. And typically, even if the business is sued, your personal assets are shielded, regardless of the outcome. (However, depending on the circumstances, someone who feels injured may nevertheless choose to sue you personally on the theory that you and the business were both separate wrongdoers.)

LLCs can have a single owner (single-member LLC), or there can be multiple owners (multi-member LLC) – in fact, there is no limit to the number of owners an LLC can add.

In a single-member LLC, the profits of the business are passed through to your personal income taxes without facing additional corporate taxes, which keeps things simple. For a multi-member LLC, consult an accountant, but often the LLC can file taxes as a partnership. In this case, the business files tax paperwork as an entity and the owners are issued a K-1 for any profits, which they report on their personal income tax filing. As with all tax matters, however, be sure to seek professional advice. For example, some states and localities may impose taxes on any form of business, such as a city business privilege tax. These may not be huge for large businesses, but they can be unpleasant surprises for small ones.

Overall, the governance and paperwork requirements for an LLC are lighter than they are for an S corporation or C corporation. You have more flexibility in how you divide profits and no requirements to, for example, have a board of directors, hold an annual meeting, or keep minutes of that meeting.

One final consideration – we'll talk later about preparing your company for exit, but many potential purchasers prefer to buy C corporations. However, an LLC and other businesses can be converted to C corporations in preparation for a sale, so this may not need consideration initially.

Corporations

In the United States, there are several types of corporations – C corporations, S corporations, B corporations, etc. For professionals, there are also professional corporations, or PCs. These are created under state law, but subject to IRS rules, so the process also calls for legal advice to be sure the filing and update requirements are met.

Unlike an LLC or a sole proprietorship, a corporation is an entity that's entirely separate from its owners. It has its own legal rights: It can buy or sell property; it can sue or be sued. Corporations can also raise money by selling stock (subject to securities law restrictions), opening up some attractive paths to capital.

Incorporating as a C- or S-corp provides the highest level of risk protection to the founders and owners in terms of debt and legal liability. It also provides some risk protection to the business. Even if the company founder dies or leaves the business, the business remains a going concern.

Due to its status as a separate entity, a corporation pays income tax on its profits. Often, those profits are taxed twice: First when the company makes a profit, and then again when dividends are paid to shareholders and are reported on their personal income taxes.

Incorporating brings with it a raft of governance, documentation, operational processes, and tax requirements – most of which are beyond the scope of this book.

But, from a high level, corporations are the best structure for medium- or high-risk businesses, businesses that need to raise money, or businesses that expect to be sold. Just be prepared to meet the paperwork and governance requirements.

Insurance

All this talk about risk brings up a related piece of advice: Make sure you have proper business insurance. Even with an incorporated business, you may also want to consider appropriate personal umbrella insurance coverage.

No one plans for things to go wrong, but it's wise to be prepared. Someone you employ could have a car accident on a business trip. You may be hacked in a way that leads to a data breach. A contract dispute with a client might turn ugly.

There are many reputable companies offering business insurance, often starting at very reasonable prices. A good agent will suggest a policy with coverage that's in line with the size and nature of your business and that fits your budget.

One piece of advice Kirsten has heard is to ask the agent, "If my insurance budget was a little bigger, what would you suggest that I add? And if my insurance budget was a little smaller, what would you suggest that I remove?"

There's some good news when it comes to company infrastructure: Once you have these key pieces set up in a way that supports your business, there's not much else to do.

Check periodically to make sure your decisions are still serving your needs, consulting with trusted advisors as needed.

Now that you've got your product or service chosen, picked a specialty, and set up your company's legal structure, it's time to bring in the support systems. Let's discuss how we get by...

CHAPTER 6

With a Little Help from Our Friends...

The Beatles were right when they sang, "Oh, I get by with a little help from my friends." In business, and in life, troubles are halved and celebrations are doubled when shared with your friends. Sometimes, friends are just that – supporters who listen to you and provide feedback. Other times, friends become business partners, clients, and people who help to form strategic alliances that move your business forward.

No matter what size company you're starting – from solo to conglomerate – there are ways to lighten the burden so you can be free to do what you do best.

Going Out on Your Own Doesn't Need to Mean Going Alone

Americans love the myth of the cowboy. The cowboy oozes confidence and doesn't need anybody as he drives cows across the plains. While you *can* try to run your business like a cowboy, as a one-person band, in our experience that is an extremely limiting choice. Rather than go it alone, think about how to have the people around you help, whether they are paid or unpaid.

Advisors, Lawyers, and Accountants

There are only so many hours in the day and, as an entrepreneur, a big part of your job will be marketing, making sales, and completing projects. It doesn't make sense to spend your time doing the bookkeeping and corporate filings, especially if you don't have expertise in those areas. This ties into the often-overlooked concept of opportunity cost. You may think you are saving money by doing the bookkeeping and other administrative work, but if the $1,000 you save costs you $10,000 in sales you could have generated in that time, you have a $9,000 opportunity cost.

Put in the effort early on to find good advisors. Small business lawyers and accountants can save you enormous amounts of time, effort, and heartbreak. In the beginning, it can be hard to find the money to pay advisors. This is an area in which many entrepreneurs try to scrimp, but it is "penny wise and pound foolish" as the British say. This expression warns that it is a poor choice to save tiny amounts of money now with the consequence of paying a whole lot more later.

Joe spent no time on the legal and accounting matters in his business; these were handled by outside experts. This allowed him to put more time into writing, speaking, and networking, where he could add the most value.

Kirsten, on the other hand, handled the day-to-day finance tasks for far longer than she should have. When she decided that she wanted help, it proved surprisingly hard to find the right resource.

The first bookkeeping company she brought on talked a big game about supporting start-ups but turned out to be mystified by the way her company billed for projects. The second solution was a virtual bookkeeping service that could keep her financial books and records but couldn't help with accounts payable, payroll, or invoicing and accounts receivable. The third bookkeeping company she hired did a great job with invoicing and accounts receivables, but they did her accounting in such a convoluted way that the financial documents lost all value as business tools. Finally, she moved her business to a fourth bookkeeper and all the pieces fell into place (once she also added a tax resource and a fractional CFO to get the full support she needed). Sometimes, hiring a professional resource works the first time –

other times, you need to go through a few different options before you find the right one.

Remember that if you're a consultant in the compliance space, you're selling your knowledge and experience. By using good lawyers, accountants, and advisors, you're taking advantage of others' specialty knowledge, which is good business for everyone.

Things to Consider

When hiring an advisor, consider the following:

- How did you learn of the advisor? Is it a reliable source?
- What are the reviews like?
- Can you contact any current clients to get a reference check?
- Is the level of service what you need?
- Does the advisor specialize in handling businesses of your size and kind?
- Does the advisor respond promptly?
- Are you comfortable working with this person?

There's an old story of a woman who can hear a leak in the pipes and can see the water but doesn't know how to fix it. After trying to solve the issues for several hours, she calls a plumber who comes in, takes one look at the setup, fixes it in five minutes, and gives her a bill for $250. Astonished, she says, "You only spent five minutes! Why is that worth $250?!" The plumber responds, "Because it took me 10 years to be able to fix your problem in five minutes." Use other people's expertise. You'll be glad you did.

Partnerships

Many companies begin as partnerships. Others grow organically by bringing in people who co-own part of the business. Both Kirsten and Kristy started their businesses with 100% ownership but, over time, realized that the business would strongly benefit from bringing in other people who were just as invested as they were in building the business.

In 2015, when she started Spark Compliance, Kristy knew she wanted to tap her network in America. Kristy grew up in America, went to college and law school in America, and had a large network of friends and colleagues in America. The trouble was she wasn't in America, she was in London. As she quickly found out, many companies were unwilling to hire a firm that was not in their geography.

A few months later, Kristy was approached by a former colleague at the law firm she'd worked for who was interested in moving from law into compliance consulting. Kristy brought in the partner to grow the business in the US. The business grew quickly once there was a physical presence on the ground in the States. "Having a partner in the US meant that we could bill ourselves as a multinational company, even though there were only two of us at the time," said Kristy. "It helped us to punch way above our weight and created a perception of enormous growth and breadth. Perception is reality, and the fact that we were on two continents was key to our success."

Getting Bigger

Kirsten's thinking on partnerships was strongly influenced by *The Founder's Dilemmas: Anticipating and Avoiding the Pitfalls That Can Sink a Start-Up, by Harvard Business School professor Noam Wasserman.*[2]

She read it in 2017, when she was still a solo founder with a business that had grown too big to manage with her current team. Initially, she experimented with bringing in entry-level help, like accounting students, writers who wanted to try marketing, and online virtual assistants. While inexpensive financially, these resources proved time-consuming to direct and their work needed extra review.

Wasserman's book, which is based on a decade of research into thousands of start-ups and their founders, covers key decisions, like:

- Do I start a company by myself or attract co-founders?

- If I bring in others, what are the right relationships, roles, and rewards?

As Wasserman puts it, one of the first questions you need to answer is "do I want to be rich, or do I want to be king?"

There's no right or wrong answer – people have different motivations and goals in starting a business. But you need to make sure your answer is aligned with the kind of business you want to have.

"King" founders hire no co-founders or weak co-founders. Often the people they hire are personal connections, like friends or family members – people they trust, rather than people who are best suited for the job.

The upside for a king is that they retain total control — all decisions run through them. (In Kirsten's experience, kings are often highly talented people whose work product really is above and beyond what most people offer. There's a reason they want to be king!) The downside is that the company can't grow much beyond that one person's personal work capacity and talents.

"Rich" (or "scale/growth/impact") founders take the opposite path. They hire strong co-founders and work hard to identify the very best person for the job. They are generous with equity and other rewards, giving their team a strong personal incentive to see the business succeed. They hire senior people to whom they can confidently delegate even high-level decisions – and then they get out of the way and let them do their work.

"Scale" founders give up control. Decisions get made without their input – even on major topics. They may even, one day, be replaced by another CEO if that's best for the business.

The upside is that a business which takes a scale approach can grow far beyond the founder's individual abilities. While more people can introduce more complexity, many minds working together can better solve problems because they can draw on a larger range of perspectives and experiences. Businesses founded by teams tend to grow faster and survive longer.

As Kirsten discovered, having a scale business is less lonely! Starting a business alone can be an all-consuming endeavor. When you're wrestling with big decisions, you may not have many sounding boards to turn to.

Starting a business with a co-founder or team means you're in it together – you win together and lose together, strictly on the merits of the choices you make. Going through this kind of experience can lead to a strong personal bond, which is its own reward.

After reading Wasserman's book, Kirsten made it a priority to identify and hire a high-level, highly-talented management team and give each of them a personal stake in helping to grow the business. This fundamentally changed the nature of Rethink's business and accelerated its growth trajectory. "Frankly, it was such a good decision that I sometimes can't believe I had the foresight to make it so early," Kirsten says. "This would be a very different business today if I had continued down a solo path."

Giving Up Equity

Although it was easy for Kirsten, many entrepreneurs struggle with whether to give up a percentage of their company (known as "equity" or "shares") to try to grow the business through partnership. There are advantages and disadvantages to bringing on an equity partner.

On the Plus Side

On the plus side, bringing in a partner can mean that your ability to grow is doubled. Many clients are concerned with having a single point of failure, so having more than one consultant or partner can make clients more comfortable. Having a partner also makes potential clients see that your company is truly a company, which can allow you to boost your rates and take on larger projects.

Partnerships can be fun, as the partners work hand-in-hand to make the business great. Feeling like someone has your back can give you courage and strength when things get hard. The emotional support of a good partner is invaluable.

It is also nice to have someone with whom to share ideas. Talking to people outside the company about the company's strategy can be tricky and sometimes dangerous from a trade secret and antitrust perspective. Having someone to bounce ideas off frequently makes for a stronger company.

The emotional support of a good partner is invaluable.

On the Minus Side

Partnerships can be great, but they can also be devastating if they don't work out. Studies show at least half of all partnerships fail. Partners frequently have different visions for the business, which can cause tremendous strife. If one partner is perceived not to be pulling their weight, the others may find themselves resentful. Life changes, such as getting married, having children, dealing with sick or ailing parents, or moving to a new city may create titanic shifts in how one partner wants to live or how much time they want to dedicate to the business. Partners are people, and sometimes they get bored with having a business or realize that they can make more money with a traditional job. This can cause real stress.

If a partnership goes bad, the breakdown of the relationship can feel like a divorce. There will be money spent on lawyers, angry conversations, and buy-outs that can reach hundreds of thousands or millions of dollars.

Things to Consider

Partnerships can be terrific, but if you're considering having a partner, think through the answers to each of these questions before tying the knot:

- Does the potential partner have the same vision for the company?
- Does the potential partner think the same way you do about business?
- Does the potential partner want to work approximately the same amount of time that you do in the business?
- Will the potential partner buy into the business, and if so, at what amount?
- Will the potential partner be providing sweat equity, and if so, with what expectations?

- Does the potential partner bring skills that you don't have such that you complement each other?
- What contacts does the potential partner have that will grow the business?
- How much equity does the potential partner want in order to join the company?
- How much equity are you willing to give away to bring in a potential partner?
- Will you put the potential partner on a vesting schedule, meaning that the potential partner will have to work several months or years to obtain all of the shares on offer? And if so, is the potential partner comfortable with that?

While all these considerations are valuable, perhaps the most important question is *do I really, really like this person*? This is frequently known as the airport test. If you can see yourself spending four hours at the airport with this person when a flight is delayed, that is a strong indication that the partnership has possibilities.

Keep in mind that, depending on the circumstances and what you are looking for, there is the option of having a "silent partner," or someone who is primarily a financial investor and not an active partner. In corporate terms, this can be the equivalent of offering preferred shares. The person may come first in the distribution of proceeds from the sale, but not have a say in management decisions.

In the case of Integrity Interactive Corporation, when Joe and his colleagues brought in their major equity investor, this person bought preferred shares, which meant they did not control management decisions but benefitted financially when the business was sold.

If you choose to form a partnership (whether in a partnership structure or as members of an LLC), be absolutely certain to contact a lawyer to set up the corporate structure and to create a shareholder/partnership agreement that clearly sets out what happens if one of the partners/owners chooses to leave the company. The share buy-back process is an important consideration. You don't want to have a person walking around with a piece of your company who doesn't work there any longer and may have a bitter taste in their mouth. Having ex-partners with ownership can cause problems in obtaining funding and in selling the company. Get a good lawyer to help from the beginning. This holds true even if you are a lawyer. The old adage is true – a lawyer who represents himself has a fool for a client.

Sweat Equity vs. Buy-In

When it comes to gaining ownership shares, partners tend to either buy into the firm or put in "sweat equity," which means working to build the business in exchange for ownership.

Sweat equity is easy to understand. The new partner comes to work, sometimes for free or for a very reduced salary/fee, and builds the company with the hope and expectation that they will grow with the firm, make more money over time, and eventually have a large pay-out if the company sells. It's important to consider how much equity is appropriate to give up. If you and your partner are starting the firm together from scratch, 50/50 may be appropriate. If the partner comes in once the business has started, you'll need to consider what is acceptable to you and your new partner. There is also the possibility of each partner receiving a higher percentage of revenue for the work they bring in, rather than merely taking this into account for purposes of determining equity shares.

Buying into a business can be a bit trickier than offering sweat equity. Buying in typically happens after the company is successfully up and running. If you are considering adding a new partner, typically the existing owner(s) order a valuation of the company, which will be performed by an outside group. The group will consider the company's revenue, debt, market exposure, and other factors that would affect sales price if the business were to be sold. The valuation will drive the amount that each share costs. For instance, if a new partner wants to buy 10% of the shares, and the company's valuation is $100,000, they would pay $10,000.

Having a partner is quite different from having an employee who will expect to be paid on time and consistently for the work performed. Partners often share the financial burden and consequences of up-and-down cash flow, which means you have more flexibility in managing the finances of the business. However, giving up equity can be uncomfortable, so the potential partnership needs to be robust to ensure it is worth it for you in the long run.

Despite these concerns, Joe is a huge fan of partnerships. He'll often say, "I'd rather have a small amount of something huge than full ownership of something small." This can also apply to giving employees equity incentives so that they can earn some element of ownership for their work. If this energizes their performance, then all partners end up with a greater amount, even though their percentage ownership is reduced.

Strategic Alliances

There are ways to build your business with others that don't involve sharing equity. One way to do this is with strategic alliances.

The compliance industry is a relatively small place, and working together with businesses that don't directly compete with yours can be a great boost to your visibility and referral base. If you're a consultant, you may want to work with companies that provide software or other support services but don't offer professional advisory services.

As an example, early on in Spark Compliance's existence, Kristy was approached by one of the major due diligence vendors. The company knew it didn't want the expense of offering a full-time advisory service, but it also knew that its clients frequently needed help in implementing its products or having third-party program reviews. The vendor formed an alliance with Spark Compliance, with Spark acting as the vendor's exclusive consulting partner. The alliance has proven tremendously successful: The vendor's clients get world-class advice, while Spark Compliance is introduced to more and more potential clients.

Consider whether this type of strategic alliance can work for you and your company. Not only can such alliances create business, but they can also provide additional avenues of advertising and create cross-referrals that benefit both businesses.

If you're not sure where to start in finding a strategic alliance, look at the exhibit hall of any major compliance-related conference, such as the Society of Corporate Compliance & Ethics (SCCE) Compliance & Ethics Institute. Get to know the leaders in compliance training, communications, risk management, third-party due diligence, and other platforms. If there is a good match, see if a formal alliance can be formed. These can easily be win/win situations that bolster your business.

The Potential Perils

Kristy was surprised to find that within months of starting Spark Compliance, many companies approached her with the offer of referral bonuses. She considered each offer, ultimately deciding not to participate. "Companies trust me to be impartial in my advice. If I'm getting a referral bonus, I'd feel a need to disclose this conflict of interest. It has the potential to create ill-will in the industry and to threaten my credibility. Ultimately, Spark Compliance has declined all such relationships." What about the relationship with the due diligence vendor? That relationship does not include referral bonuses, so the potential conflict does not exist.

If you've started a company that doesn't require you to be impartial in your advice, creating alliances that offer referral bonuses can be a boon to your bottom line. Recommending products that you believe in, and that your clients need, can be a fulfilling experience. It can also help your clients to trust you more if you solve their problems with introductions to technologies or products that make their program better.

Find Your Team

Whether they become formal partners, strategic advisors, mentors, or friends, finding people with whom to collaborate is a key to true success. Reid Hoffman, the founder of LinkedIn, said it best: "No matter how brilliant your mind or strategy, if you're playing a solo game, you'll always lose out to a team."

CHAPTER 7

Capital: Financing Your Big Dream

What do you think is the biggest risk to your business? Being beaten to market by the competition? Failing to deliver the best product? Having your website go down? Nope – far and away the biggest risk to your business is running out of money. It may surprise you to find out that many successful businesses shut every year because they can't find enough cash to keep going. How can that be? It's all well and good to have $200,000 in receivables due in 90 days, but if you can't pay your staff (or yourself) *now*, that money doesn't matter – you'll be out of business before it comes in.

In our experience, failure to recognize the importance of capital is one of the most common stumbling blocks of going into business. Kristy readily admits that she didn't anticipate the financial strain of creating Spark Compliance. The company had a cash crisis a few months in. Had it not been for an unexpected bonus from her prior job, she might not have been able to weather the early storm. That painful lesson was vital to the ultimate success of Spark Compliance. Now that she knows that cash is crucial, Kristy and her management team review a spreadsheet noting all expenses and expected payments for the next 12 weeks, which is updated weekly. "We'll never again be in the situation where the business could go under for lack of cash flow. If we can see the issue 12 weeks out, we can plan for it. I didn't understand how to do that when I started Spark."

In this chapter, we'll go through what you need to do to prepare financially to start your company. We'll discuss the various places where money can be obtained, and the pros and cons of each approach. We'll also consider what happens after you start, with advice on how to make things go more smoothly.

Preparation Is Key

Joe was more prepared than most to start his business. He had worked in the corporate world for 20 years and took advantage of every opportunity to save. He chose to automatically move money into savings and investments before he could get his hands on it. When he left the corporate nest, he had his two children's college accounts fully funded and his mortgage paid off. He also had a retirement fund from his corporate job.

In a sense, Joe had the chance to get paid while helping to develop the new field of compliance and ethics that became his career. But if fully funding your retirement and children's college funds will leave you 20 years older before starting your business, there are other ways to prepare financially to capitalize your company.

What's in Your Wallet?

The more money you have, the more runway you'll have. "Runway" is a term used in the start-up world to describe the amount of time between now and when a company will run out of money. "Burn rate" is the speed at which that money is devoured. If you have $100,000 in the bank and your burn rate is $10,000 per month, you have ten months of runway. The more money you have, the longer your runway.

Personal Debt

In an ideal world, you'd be entirely out of personal debt before starting your business. Realistically, the more debt you can pay down before starting the business, the better. But sometimes conserving cash is more important than paying down debt. Kristy deferred her law school student loan payments for the first six months of Spark's existence. "I wanted to conserve cash in any way possible. The interest rates on my student loans were between 2.5 and 6%. The cash was more important in the short term." (She's since paid off her student loans entirely.)

If you have debt, look for ways to consolidate it or to make the payments less onerous. You can also look to cut back your bills or defer payments while the business is new.

In the critical early days of a business, being professionally and personally frugal will buy you time. Look carefully at your personal and business expenses and consider what you can cut. Are there subscriptions or services you can cancel? Can you go with the free website builder rather than hire a pro to do it for you? Every dollar you can keep in your pocket is a dollar you wait to collect from a client— and there may be weeks and months when you need the margin.

How Much Do I Need?

The type of business that you choose to operate will have a significant effect on how much money you'll need to begin. If you're looking to start a software company, that will take significantly more capital than starting a solo consulting practice out of your home.

Ideally, you'd have six months of personal expenses and at least three months of business expenses saved up before hanging your shingle. This is because it may take longer than you think to get your first client, and even when you do, getting paid can be a challenge.

Let's say you have a start-up that will provide the best new policy management software on the market. You estimate that to build the software, you'll need two developers. To sell the software, you'll need to hire one salesperson. You then determine that you'll also need a finance person to manage the business side of the business. Now let's say the software takes two months to build, and in month three, you get your first client. Congratulations! There's just one thing – it may take two months to negotiate the contract for signature. After the negotiation, you may have to wait until after you implement the software to send the first invoice, which may take 60 more days to be paid by the company. Suddenly it's six months later and you've not been paid a dime.

Remember, most of the time, employees are paid on a monthly or bimonthly basis. They aren't going to be interested in waiting until your first big client's payments come in. If you have employees, you will need the capital to pay them weeks or months before you yourself are paid anything at all.

In solo consulting, when you win a contract, you usually have to do at least one month's work before you can send your invoice, and even then, with most contracts, payment is due a minimum of 30 days later. That's a minimum of 60 days from the start of a project to payment.

Undercapitalization is dangerous, but you can mitigate the risk by ensuring you have enough capital when you start.

Sources of Capital

Many people never fulfill their dreams of starting a business because they don't personally have the cash to do it. But the truth is that there are many sources of capital available. Each of these sources has its pros and cons. How do you finance your dream? Try one or more of the following:

Personal Savings

Personal savings allow you to spend your money any way you choose – a luxury you do not have with most other sources of capital. Personal savings allow you to "bootstrap" – that is, to fund your company as you go.

On the positive side, if you fund your company with personal savings, you will not be financially beholden to anyone. You can make your own decisions, choose the clients and projects that you like, and spend more time building the company than you would otherwise be able to do. If you happen to have another breadwinner in the family who shares your vision, you may also have more flexibility and staying power.

On the negative side, personal savings can dwindle fast, putting you personally in a precarious situation. You will not have others to lean on in the same way you might be able to with alternative funding. Personal savings are critical when you start but may not be the best way to fund your company.

Partnerships

As discussed in detail in other sections of the book, partnerships with individuals and other companies can be a great (or horrible) thing. In terms of capital, many times partners bring significant amounts of money to the table. When you're starting up, a business partner may provide capital in return for shares or a percentage of ownership in the company. Human capital is frequently as important as financial capital, so this can be a great boon.

Start-Up Loans

Many government and quasi-governmental agencies want to support start-up businesses. You can search out the small business administration in your country, state, province, city, or town to see if start-up loans are available.

Kristy went to Virgin StartUp to get her seed capital. Virgin StartUp was created to support entrepreneurship in Britain. Loans up to £25,000 ($35,000 or so) were available for the right project. Kristy applied for a £7,500 loan, which would only be awarded if she could survive the multi-month process of proving her idea.

The first step in the Virgin process was attending a *Shark Tank*-style event where entrepreneurs seeking funding pitched their ideas to the Virgin StartUp leaders. Next, she had to draft an in-depth business plan. The plan had to include evidence proving that there was a gap in the market or that a market existed that needed the product or service. This meant that Kristy had to send out a survey to 100 compliance officers asking them what type of consulting services they were interested in, and how their current providers were failing them. The information she obtained proved invaluable. It also allowed her to share with 100 potential customers that she'd be opening her own firm shortly.

After all of that, Kristy had to convince a Virgin-affiliated business coach that she was "ready" to graduate into business with the loan from Virgin. Kristy was given the green light three weeks before she was scheduled to open Spark Compliance. "The money was nice, but it was a small loan that did not provide much runway. The real benefit of the Virgin process was learning how to think like an entrepreneur. They required a lot, but the benefit of completing the tasks was immeasurable."

Start-up loans can be enormously beneficial because they normally come with low interest rates. You also don't have to give up shares/equity in your company to get them. The downside is that they may take quite a bit of time to get, and all that time may be for naught if the loan isn't ultimately approved. Lastly, loans come with a repayment schedule. Saddling your company with a loan before it even starts can quickly strain it.

Family and Friends

Another route is to ask family or friends for the money to start your business. This is a common way of funding a new company, but it can be fraught with emotional risk. Parents or your rich uncle may be willing to gift you the money, but most of the time, it will be loaned to you for a period of time.

If you choose to take money from family or friends, be sure to write up a loan agreement with a repayment schedule and a fair interest rate. Treat the money as if it were from a bank or credit card company. Losing your business is nothing compared to losing relationships with those you love. Ultimately, if the business fails, loans can be discharged in bankruptcy; guilt with family and friends cannot.

Selling Things

Need capital fast and have a collection of watches or rare coins? You can always sell them to capitalize your business. People have sold investment properties, cars, stocks, and all sorts of personal effects to finance their business. On the plus side, you can get fast cash for selling your assets. On the downside, you will no longer have the asset, and if the business tanks, you'll be out of both your business and your assets.

Credit Cards and Lines of Credit

Many people use debt to finance the start of their company. People sometimes use personal credit cards or lines of credit (including home equity loans) to finance their businesses. This is a high-risk strategy, since credit cards typically have astronomically high interest rates, and an unpaid line of credit could cause your home to be foreclosed and sold out from under you. Nevertheless, using these financial instruments to manage short-term cash flow issues can be an effective, if dangerous, strategy. It certainly provides an intense level of motivation to succeed.

In Kirsten's case, in the early days of Rethink, she paid for many company expenses with an American Express Starwood credit card (now Marriott Bonvoy). This let her delay payment by 30 days or more – and she used the points earned to book free or cheap hotel rooms for business trips. Carrying a sizable balance did, however, have a temporary impact on her personal credit score.

Once the company has reached a certain size and can demonstrate stability, it's also possible to qualify for lines of credit with banks at more favorable rates than credit cards. Until the business is quite large, however, most require the owner's personal guarantee – which means that you are personally on the hook for the balance if the company can't meet its obligations.

Start-Up Investors

Individual investors that are only interested in a return on their money may be willing to buy part of your company early on. These types of investors usually do not want to run the day-to-day business.

They may be family or friends who take equity instead of loaning you the money, or they may be wealthy people in your community that want to invest in your idea. On the plus side, this money usually comes without the requirement of paying it back. On the downside, giving away pieces of your company early on can leave you with little equity when your company grows, making it difficult to take on new investors because you don't have much stock left to give in exchange for more funds.

Banks and Commercial Loans

For at least the first year, businesses are typically unable to secure traditional bank loans. However, once you have a track record of a few years in business, banks become significantly more willing to offer loans. Bank loans can help you to bridge cash flow issues or to invest in new staff, technology, or marketing activities. Keep in mind, though, that loan repayments may be a drag on cash flow for several years. Nevertheless, when starting your business and selecting a bank, consider the long-term potential for developing a relationship with that bank that could include financing down the road.

Angels, Private Equity, and Venture Capital

Once you have a successful business with good cash flow or high-growth capacity, you will likely be courted by sophisticated investors that want to put money into your business in exchange for stock or partial ownership.

An "angel" is one investor of this type. Angel investors are typically high net-worth individuals looking for a place to park their money with the potential for higher returns than they'd get in the stock market or traditional investments. An angel often aids the business by offering both money and business expertise as an advisor.

In Joe's case, the capital for Integrity Interactive came through a phone call. As explained in Joe's Entrepreneurial Story, he had spent years networking with people in the corporate world. When he and Kirk Jordan started Integrity Interactive and brought in Carl Nelson, they all realized the company needed capital. As fate would have it, Joe got a call from an acquaintance named Jim asking if Joe knew of anywhere to invest in the nascent online training field. When Joe explained that he and Carl were starting a company, Jim responded, "That's why I called you – I knew you would know where to invest."

Jim flew out to Integrity's Boston area headquarters, kicked the tires and ran the numbers, and then had his company invest $500,000 for preferred stock. As it worked out, this was all the capital the company ever needed – and it was by far the best investment Jim ever made.

In addition to angels, there may be interest in your company from various types of aggressive pooled-fund investment groups. These types of companies, often called private equity funds, family offices, and venture capital funds, tend to look for high-growth (frequently technology-driven or software-based) companies in which they invest for a fast return.

On the plus side, large investment funds or wealthy individuals may provide capital to achieve big goals much more quickly than bootstrapping. On the negative side, such money may require giving up substantial equity. Sometimes these pooled-fund investors may take control of the company, leaving you with a minority share and less of a voice about how the business is run. They may also have unrealistic expectations about the growth potential of the company, which can create enormous amounts of stress for the entrepreneur.

Crowdfunding Platforms

In recent years, online funding platforms have come into the lending space that used to be reserved for banks. Companies like Funding Circle, Zopa, and Lending Club all offer loans to businesses funded by members that receive a set return on their investment. You win because the loans don't require you to give up equity. The downside is that you'll need to pay the loan back each month, which contributes to higher expenses in the long-term.

If you have a unique product, you can try to get it crowdfunded through platforms like Kickstarter. If enough people are interested in your product, and you can pre-sell it up to the reserve amount, you'll get the investment and have immediate clients. Products in the compliance market don't tend to have broad enough appeal to complete a Kickstarter-style campaign, but you never know. It may be worth considering this route.

Factoring

Another way to obtain capital when your business is up and running is to factor your invoices.

Let's say you have a $100,000 invoice out to a large company with a poor reputation for paying on time. You need the $100,000 now, not in 90 days.

A factoring company will pay you $90,000 now, and then when the bill is paid by the large company, they'll keep the $10,000 difference as their payment. Factoring can help you to get out of a tight spot, but it reduces profit quickly. It can help but shouldn't be used frequently if you can help it.

Keeping Cash Capital Needs Down

One other key element related to capital is keeping your cash needs down. This may include working from home or finding space at a discount. In the case of Integrity Interactive, Carl Nelson knew the start-up world well. He was able to get furniture for pennies on the dollar and negotiate start-up space in a low-rent district for a fraction of what an inexperienced businessperson would pay.

Knowing where and how to shop can be a significant element in calculating capital needs. To tweak a well-known phrase, "A dollar saved is a dollar not financed."

Similarly, the cost of promoting the business is variable. If you are on the speakers' circuit working with various organizations, you may already have access to free promotional activities, plus the ability to get free continuing education credits. You may find that you can similarly promote online without incurring any marketing expenses.

You may even be able to find similar arrangements with personnel. It is possible to have family help in the business for "deferred compensation." It may also be possible to pay project rates or partner with others without having to pay them until revenue comes in.

It's Not One and Done – You'll Probably Need More as You Grow

Over the lifetime of your business, you will likely utilize multiple financing tools. You may need capital to pay for employees to help to grow the business once it is on its way. You may need capital to invest in marketing, going to conferences, or doing other sales-related activities. You may need to invest in coaching, software, or other technology to create more efficient systems as your company grows.

Spark Compliance used personal savings, partnerships, a start-up loan, and a crowdfunding loan to help it grow. Integrity Interactive was fortunate enough to get a large infusion in the beginning and then function based on a subscription revenue model. Rethink used a combination of business profits, personal savings, personal credit cards, business credit cards, factoring receivables, and a bank line of credit, taking care to move towards less risky, lower-rate options as the company grew.

The good news is that as your business grows and becomes more sophisticated, the financing options available to it will grow as well. Debt and equity financing both have their pros and cons. The trick is to choose the best financing tool for your business at the right time.

Cash Isn't the Only Capital

Lastly, remember that cash isn't the only form of capital. Resourcefulness – like bartering, trading, or using the skills of a willing friend or family member – can allow you to get what you need without breaking the bank.

SECTION TWO:
Execution

Now that you've got your company started, it's time to turn over that "Open for Business" sign. In this section, we'll look at important topics, including deciding where to work, managing clients, and making sales.

CHAPTER 8

Where do I Work?

Not that long ago, most professionals lived near their workplace and went to an office every day. But the digital revolution has brought the ability to work from anywhere and increased the number of options for where that work takes place.

When Joe joined Kirk Jordan of CSLG in 1996, the firm had a small office in Rhode Island. Joe operated separately from CSLG in his own town in another state.

"I didn't want to conduct business from my house. At the time, I was a single parent with two teenagers, so I partnered with another professional who also wanted outside space," Joe said. "We rented space together for a short period until I bought a small office building in a converted house." He then let his colleague rent space from him.

Joe found it helpful to be away from his house (and his two children), and over time had clients and other professionals visit his office. Over the years, Joe also accumulated quite a bit of professional material that was better kept away from home.

Conversely, when Kirsten founded Rethink Compliance in 2015, she kept the company virtual from the start. At that point, she had already been working remotely for six years and knew the upsides – including just how much you can get done when you remove the commute and socializing from your workday.

As the company grew, its virtual status allowed the leadership team to hire the best candidates they could find, regardless of where those people were located. By 2019, there were Rethink employees in all four major US time zones, including many who viewed the "work from home" environment as a plus.

Rethink's leadership team meets in person a few times a year to plan and strategize and often see each other at sales meetings and conferences. Each day, the team serves clients all over the world, doing work that would have been done virtually even if Rethink had a dedicated office. With clients in several US cities plus Europe and Asia, it doesn't seem strange that most in-person meetings required a flight.

"In the spring of 2020, when the world locked down in response to COVID-19, being virtual was an advantage," Kirsten said. "Despite all the general disruption, very little changed in the team's daily work life. Rethink's technology and infrastructure were already in place."

When it comes to choosing your workspace, you have a range of options, and the right answer will depend in part on your preferences, your team, your clients, and the nature of your work.

Fully Virtual

Being fully virtual has the benefit of being free, or at least cheap, depending on how much of your team's office setup you subsidize.

For many people, being fully virtual is a workplace benefit; one that allows them better work-life balance (No commute! Someone is home when your kids get off the bus! You can pop dinner in the oven at 3 p.m.!). But there are upsides to having an outside office. Joe reports that because he works from an outside office, he has never had a cat walk across the screen during an important Zoom call.

When Kirsten first started to work virtually, it was a relief. "After nearly 20 years commuting, I could simply close my computer in the afternoon and be home for the day," she said. "That said, one year into the COVID-19 lockdown, I rented an apartment to use as an office to get some much-needed separation between my home and my work. The company is still virtual, but now I have a dedicated office space. As we keep saying in this book, 'Things will change as you go!'"

But virtual work also has its downsides and complications, especially as a company grows. Some questions you should ask include:

- Have you hired people who can keep focused on work while working from home?
- Do they have a dedicated office space?
- Is their setup professional enough for client-facing conversations?
- Do your team members have the computer and other equipment they need?
- What will you do if they need support to get set up or IT support in general?
- Where will you store company materials?
- How will you share access?
- How can you ensure the business retains its information and records if someone leaves?
- Do you have adequate information privacy and security measures in place across the company? Are you sure?
- How do you build a group culture?
- How do team members get to know one another?
- How do you onboard new employees?

There are also tax implications. Here, we do not offer any professional advice; for that, you should consult your own tax professional. But we can share our experiences.

In the US, for example, you need to register to do business in every US state where you employ someone. If you have W2 employees, you need to collect and remit state income taxes at the correct rate, pay the appropriate amount to the appropriate state's unemployment compensation fund, and meet more regulatory requirements overall than if you were located in a single jurisdiction and following a single state's rules.

Depending on your corporate structure, you may also owe additional taxes to the states in which you do business or where your employees are located. So, while a multi-location virtual company can be simple to set up, it can be a headache to administer.

Fully Officed

Committing to an office lease costs money (unless, like Joe, you own the building and rent space out to other tenants). For companies strapped for cash, a lease can be a large commitment.

However, there are also real benefits to having a dedicated office for your company, including:

- A dedicated office space outside your home – no cats, dogs, or children.
- A single location for files and other information.
- Control over IT infrastructure, including security and privacy standards.
- The ability to maintain and access work product and files if someone leaves the company.
- The ability to control access to the building.
- A business address that's separate from the founder's home address.
- A business-appropriate meeting space.
- The psychological impact of "being at work" and not at home.
- The capacity to leave your office so it doesn't call to you from down the hall at night.

In Joe's case, having an office gave him a chance to meet with clients as well as handle confidential matters in a more secure environment.

"While most client meetings occurred at the client's location, there were occasions where client representatives preferred the opportunity to get out of their offices and meet in the small town where I was located," Joe said.

This was also true for others in the profession who were interested in networking and discussing other professional matters, such as writing.

Coworking Options

Thanks to WeWork and similar coworking companies, it's now possible to combine the flexibility and low financial commitment of virtual work with the benefits of a dedicated office.

In most major cities, there are dozens of coworking options, from single-location businesses to WeWork and Regus' networks of thousands of locations across the globe.

Unlike leases, which commit your business to several years of payments, coworking membership plans are flexible, often allowing you to pay month to month and cancel any time.

You can also decide how much office you need and scale as you go.

The cheapest plans might give you 10 days of access per month with a "hot seat" membership, which allows you access to (typically very nice) public working spaces with printers and fast Wi-Fi. More extensive plans allow for dedicated office space with drawers and doors that lock — for one person, for two people, or a whole team.

Companies with a coworking membership can trade up to new, bigger offices or switch between locations as their needs change. And most coworking memberships allow members to book conference rooms or other gathering spaces and to make reservations in other locations run by the same company.

As this new industry grows, it's sometimes possible to get access to coworking spaces through various benefits and perks. For example, Kirsten once got a free hotseat membership to WeWork for a year, just by signing up for an American Express Business card.

These benefits gave Kirsten a (dog-friendly!) place to occasionally work outside the house in Denver and allowed her to schedule conference rooms for meetings in Denver, Boston, and London for a reasonable hourly fee. During one trip to New York City, she was able to quickly find a quiet, Wi-Fi-enabled place to work during an unexpected break from meetings, complete with snacks and coffee.

Professional organizations may offer coworking space as well. For instance, in London, Kristy is a member of the Institute of Directors (IOD), which has a building in the center of town. Everyone in the multistory space is a business owner or director. Guests must be registered. Meeting spaces – including a restaurant, wine bar, and traditional conference rooms – are available. "The IOD building is a great place to meet with clients and to get work done between meetings in the city. Membership is worth its weight in gold," said Kristy.

No matter where you choose to work, the most important thing you'll be doing is making sales. In the next chapter, we'll dive into the ins and outs of this critical part of your business – after all, if you're not making sales, you won't be in business long!

CHAPTER 9

Sales and Client Relations

It's become a cliché in start-ups: "Everyone's in sales!"

But as you're getting a company off the ground, and then later, as you're trying to grow your client base or expand into new areas, it becomes clear that the sales process starts long before you are sitting across the table from a prospective client.

In fact, many earlier decisions and actions – including some taken long ago – contribute to whether customers are eagerly receptive or lukewarm, if they move quickly to close the deal or drag the process out, and even if they are likely to buy from you again.

In this chapter, we'll cover mindsets, tactics, and approaches for getting people to buy what you are selling.

But first, a caveat: Getting the fundamentals of your business right is by far the most powerful driver for sales, more important than any individual sales action you take or the most talented resource you can hire.

Sales start with good product and business strategy decisions:

- Are you selling something the market wants and has a budget for?
- Is there a reason to choose you over your competitors?
- Are you priced well?
- Are you talking to a prospect at the right point in the budget cycle?

- Do you have a market presence and industry credibility i.e., do people know who you are?

Getting all these elements right can lead to sales that feel almost easy — clients keep showing up with a keen interest and money to spend. Getting one or more of these elements wrong can throw sand in the gears and introduce obstacles that drag out or derail the sales process, even for interested clients.

So while this chapter is about sales techniques and tactics, your very best sales tactic is also to choose the right business model and offer great products and services in the first place.

You Aren't Selling — You're Helping People Solve Problems

There are so many negative stereotypes of salespeople. From the slimy used-car salesman to the snake oil salesperson riding into town only to be shoved out by pitchfork-wielding villagers, it's not difficult to find ugly references to selling. It's enough to make anyone hide under the covers and write blog posts instead of going out to the market to find someone who wants to pay them for their product or service.

The mindset that sales is somehow immoral or icky is utterly counterproductive for an entrepreneur. Changing that mindset is a key to success. In *Secrets of the Millionaire Mind*, author T. Harv Eker implores readers to think about sales as *helping people to solve their problems* using your product or service. He writes, "If you believe in your value, how could you possibly hide it from people who need it?" He continues, "Suppose you had the cure for arthritis and you met someone who was suffering and in pain with the disease. Would you hide it from him or her? Would you wait for that person to read your mind or guess that you have a product that could help? What would you think of someone who didn't offer suffering people the opportunity because they were too shy, too afraid, or too cool to promote?"[3]

When you change your mindset from that of forcing yourself on people to that of finding people who need the solution you have, you change the energy of the sales conversation. The shift can make rejection feel less personal. If your prospect doesn't need your solution, it isn't you that they're rejecting, it's the solution. In fact, if a person doesn't buy, that's actually a good thing, because they aren't a good fit and wouldn't have a good experience because of that lack of need.

Your job is to help people to solve their problems with your product or solution. You are doing them a favor by offering it to them, which is truly something to be proud of.

Sell Holes, Not Drills

There's a famous phrase in the sales world: "People buy holes in walls, not drills." This means that people don't buy a drill because they are aesthetically pleasing or sound nice when they're being used. People buy a drill to make a hole in the wall. They are looking for the *outcome* they desire, not the vehicle that delivers the outcome.

This concept is often called "selling the benefits, not the features." Mediocre salespeople sell the features. The best salespeople sell the benefits. How does this work? Let's say a man walks into a flower store on Valentine's Day asking for advice in buying roses. A mediocre salesperson might explain how the most expensive roses came from Kenya and were raised on the best organic soil. A great salesperson would describe how lucky and adored the man's wife will feel when she gets the very best roses – those raised in Kenya in the best organic soil. The feature is the origin of the roses. The benefit is how the wife will feel when she receives them.

How does this work in the compliance profession? If a potential client calls to ask for a risk assessment, what are they really looking for? Sure, they'd like to get your perspective on their risk and to identify places where they should be focusing their resources. But what they truly want is the confidence that their program is properly managing risk and that their decisions will be defensible if they're ever in front of a regulator or prosecutor. You're selling confidence and a sense of calm at the end of the project, not merely a lengthy report.

When in a sales conversation, always try to determine what the prospect wants. It may seem obvious that if a person is asking for compliance training courses, they want compliance training courses. But in addition to training courses, they probably want a vendor that delivers a product that makes the compliance department look good. Focus on selling benefits and you'll be much more likely to sell your products or services.

What's Your USP?

In the business world, "USP" stands for "unique selling proposition." It refers to the unique benefit exhibited by a company, product, service, or brand that helps it to stand out from competitors. Developing and defining your USP is important because it can help you to clearly differentiate why your customers should buy from you instead of the competition.

Your USP can come from many different sources. These include:

- Being the cheapest in the market.
- Having the best quality materials.
- The expertise of the people involved in creating or delivering the product or service.
- The fame of the people involved in creating or delivering the product or service.
- Great branding or advertising that resonates with the audience.
- Exclusivity.
- Stellar reputation for:
- customer service
- delivering on time
- reliability of some other sort
- Innovativeness of the product or service.

Define the characteristics that make your product, service, or brand stand out, then highlight those unique attributes in all of your marketing and brand placement. This can make sales easier to make.

Where Do I Start?

In 2016, Rethink Compliance didn't sell anything for the entire fourth quarter.

Now, there were a lot of factors in play: Kirsten had ended some consulting contracts to focus on building new, more promising lines of business. A client in the final stages of paperwork got laid off, along with 40% of that client's company, so that contract vanished. And Rethink's one sales resource took a leave of absence to deal with a parent's failing health.

Still, it was a shocking development, and Kirsten spent November seeking advice from friends and contacts who'd built sales careers. (She had plenty of time on her hands.) She and a part-time marketing resource also spent that winter building the company's first real marketing engine – and by early 2017, that marketing engine had started to deliver real inbound sales leads. It still does today – so, for completeness, this chapter on sales should be read alongside our chapters on marketing and online presence, since these elements all work together to produce a sales pipeline.

The first person Kirsten sought out for advice had led sales teams for nearly a decade. In fact, in a previous role, she had often traveled to support sales and renewal discussions for him and his team.

His advice? Start with the people you know. He told her, "You've built a 15-year career in compliance. People know you. People trust you. Start calling people – not to try to sell them something over the phone, but to let them know what you're up to."

Just Get Yourself in Front of People

An important rule of sales is this: ***Just get yourself in front of people.***

What Kirsten learned in that dark quarter of 2016 is that if you've built a product the market wants, and if you get yourself in front of enough prospective buyers to talk about it, sooner or later someone will buy what you're offering or refer you to someone who will.

This won't just happen – you have to make it happen, not just once but week after week, month after month. And the people you talk to have to be actual prospective buyers. They need to have the ability and budget to buy from you or you won't get anywhere useful.

Maybe it's calling a work contact to connect. Or telling someone you'll be in town and asking to meet. Or scheduling a meal with someone at a conference. Or asking someone you know more distantly for a call. Maybe it's looking on LinkedIn to see if any of your college alumni are in your field. Most likely, it'll be all of these things and more – repeated with as large a group of people as possible.

This is a long game, but it's a powerful one.

Planting the Seeds

Your goal isn't to make a deal during your first conversation ("What's it going to take to get you in a new car today?!"). It's very likely that you won't!

If you try to pressure people into sales before they're ready, you'll turn off your buyer and sour your network. (This is where building your personal and company financial security matters. You don't want to be desperate to make a sale — in fact, feeling like you have to sell increases the chances that you won't.)

People like to buy things but hate to be sold on them. And, especially in compliance, people only buy when they're ready, and it may take months or years. So what you are doing in all those conversations is planting seeds for a sales opportunity in the future. And you're casting a wide enough net, for a long enough time, that you start to successfully catch some clients.

For some people, this kind of sales-focused networking comes naturally. Others have to be more intentional.

In fact, intentional people are sometimes better at it because they're more consistent and deliberate. For example, when Kirsten was seeking advice on sales, she talked to an attorney who had just made partner at his law firm, largely due to his outsized business development skills. Introverted, methodical, and soft-spoken, the attorney was about as far from a natural glad-hander as you can get! But he'd developed a system that worked for him.

He told Kirsten, "Every week, without fail, I aim to make a certain number of connections. I golf with people. I go to lunch. I check in with people on the phone. And when I do that, week in and week out, and keep expanding the list of people I'm talking to, new opportunities pop up every week. They may not be related to the people I'm talking to this week. It might be someone from six or eight weeks ago. But when I do this consistently, opportunities show up consistently."

Think of your sales process as an opportunity-generating machine and build from there.

Who Is the Head of Sales?

When Kirsten started Rethink, she thought "sales" had a singular meaning: Getting leads in the door and getting business closed.

But it turns out selling is more nuanced than simply landing a big deal. It is a process, and it requires passion and talent to do it well.

As the founder of the company, you either need to hire and manage the head of sales or be the head of sales. You need to hunt for sales or attract them some other way – or both. No matter what, the buck stops with you.

The Founder's Advantage

When you set out to sell as a company founder, you actually have a huge advantage.

This is something a mentor told Kirsten back when Rethink was getting ready to staff its first booth at a compliance conference.

At that point, her friend had built a 20-year sales career focused solely on hunting and lead generation. He was so talented that, for a while, he ran a company whose sole purpose was to generate leads and set meetings for other businesses.

"Showing up as the founder is a huge advantage," he told her. "Every other booth just has some dumb sales guy like me standing there. You know the product. You do the hands-on work. You're the person that your clients want to talk to."

And he was right.

A founder might be an amateur when it comes to sales tactics and techniques, but she might make up for any inexperience by knowing the field inside and out and being absolutely passionate about the business.

Even when the company grows large enough to step away from the day-to-day sales, clients often want to talk to the CEO before they sign a big deal. So even when you're no longer the head of sales, you may still be a key part of the sales team.

Kristy has found this to be true. "People tend to want to talk to me and to know that I will be part of their project. It can be hard to introduce others in my company to new clients because I've made myself the face of the business. But, ultimately, I have to pass large parts of our projects on to others because I need to focus strongly on having more conversations that lead to more sales to grow the business."

Should You Hire a Salesperson?

In a start-up, sales are scrappy. Everything is about results, about getting in front of potential clients to generate new business out of nothing. And not everyone knows how to do this – including people who've been in "sales" for decades.

People think of salespeople as those who work the phones cold-calling potential customers all day long looking for a hot lead. In fact, in many established businesses, sales is more about working inbound leads and renewing existing customers. Many successful career salespeople never actually generate a lead or work hard to develop a lukewarm introduction into something more promising. They simply nurture the customers they have and guide potential ones who want to buy.

What good salespeople do is a real skill, and you may need a good salesperson or sales team when you're a bigger business. But when you start out, you may be your own best resource for getting sales.

What Great Salespeople Do (Whether You or Someone Else)

The "how" of sales will vary quite a bit among companies. A consulting sale is different from a product sale. A sales channel that works for one type of company or founder might fall flat for another. Regardless, there are endless amounts of books, training courses, and workshops to help you develop your sales skills.

So, in this section, we're going to focus instead on some qualities that set great salespeople apart. These are drawn from a *Harvard Business Review* article called "The 5 Things All Great Salespeople Do."[4]

The author, Joseph Curtis, wrote the article after spending 16 years in technology sales and sales leadership, including for Salesforce. Here's his list:

The best salespeople own everything

His point? Your success depends on you. In other words, if something happens "it may not be [your] fault, but it is [your] responsibility." Sure, your client got laid off and the deal got canceled. Now, what are you going to do to get the next 10 deals?

The best salespeople are resourceful

Whether it's working their personal and professional networks, finding ways to get a speaking slot at conferences, figuring out how to have a booth in a conference exhibit hall on a shoestring budget, or finding free or cheap advertising channels, great salespeople find a way. As Curtis says, "Resourcefulness is as much a mindset as it is a skill."

The best salespeople are experts

Curtis lends insight into why company founders can be so effective at selling: "Sales is less about selling and more about leading, which requires high levels of confidence, which in turn requires knowledge and experience." This confidence can take years to acquire – and, once you have it, gives you an edge on anyone selling into your industry without it.

The best salespeople help others

This is a very interesting insight. Throughout this book, we've talked about seeking to add value – and, as it turns out, great salespeople do this naturally, in ways that seem to return value to them over the long run. As Curtis says, "The best salespeople I have observed regularly pass their knowledge on to less tenured or less experienced salespeople with no expectation of anything in return."

The best salespeople move quickly

Urgency matters in sales! The best salespeople show the client that they are actually interested in doing business with them – something they signal just by answering promptly. Kirsten once participated in a request for proposal (RFP) where Rethink was the only company to return its proposal on time. Two of the companies that failed to respond then called after the deadline to ask if the deadline could be extended. (The client was happy to turn them down.)

Not surprisingly, these sales traits are also excellent qualities for an entrepreneur! Kirsten has found the above list to be a good reference when hiring anyone into a start-up, not just salespeople.

Pricing

When starting a business, one crucial question is what to charge. This can seem like a simple issue to solve, but it usually isn't. Pricing is an art and not a science.

One useful consideration is where you want to position yourself in the market in terms of price. Every market has high- and low-end offerings, and the compliance and ethics world is no different. If your price is too high, you won't have any customers. If your price is too low, prospective purchasers may be turned off and not buy because they fear poor quality.

Before Spark Compliance opened its doors, Kristy knew how she wanted it positioned. "I wanted Spark Compliance to compete with the big law firms and huge accounting companies that had expanded into the compliance market. I had worked in a big law firm for years and had been a customer to the big accounting firms when I was in-house, so I had a good sense of their pricing. Spark Compliance's hourly pricing is less than theirs without being too inexpensive. We went for the juxtaposition of very high-end, boutique service with a pricing point that puts us in the middle of the market."

Kristy admits that it took some tinkering to get it right. She knew she'd hit the sweet spot when some potential clients turned her down for being too expensive, and others asked why her proposals were so much cheaper than that from the big law/ consulting firms vying for the same job.

Joe notes that at Integrity Interactive, they had the good fortune to have a major competitor that charged an extremely high flat rate for its services. Since Integrity was in the market before online training was considered more of a commodity, their competitor's high prices gave sufficient room to choose lower prices that still gave them good margins and the ability to provide value for money. Integrity Interactive wasn't the first in the market, but since its products had added features missing from the biggest player at a significantly lower cost, they had their USP.

The Elements of Price

Many considerations go into choosing a good price for your products and services. Some things you should think about include:

Material Costs

The first element of pricing is the cost of materials. If your deliverables are all online or come in a PDF report, this element may be negligible. However, if you have a physical product, be sure to cover the cost of the things that make up your product in the price presented to the client.

Your Time

People tend to think of their time as being free when they are employees. After all, they have to be at the office eight hours per day, so who cares if a task takes an hour or six days? Entrepreneurs must think differently. Even if you're a consultant charging an hourly rate, there are only so many hours any client will be willing to pay for when it comes to their projects, so estimate properly when considering this element.

Others' Time

If you are using sub-contractors or employees at your company to service the client, consider their time. Remember that you will want to make a premium on the cost of others' time. In other words, if your sub-contractor makes $100 per hour from you, you'll likely want to charge more than $100 in your price to cover that cost. One rule of thumb when using others' time is this: Charge three times whatever you're paying the individual. If you're paying $100 to your sub-contractor, charge $300 to the client. This will allow for $100 for the sub-contractor, $100 for overhead/running the business, and $100 in profit. Speaking of overhead...

Overhead

When people see the hourly rate some consultants charge, their eyes get wide. When the number is hundreds of dollars per hour (or more than $1,000 for some very high-end lawyers), employees consider quitting their jobs on the spot.

While the hourly rate can seem large, it must cover the costs of everything it takes to run a business, often known as overhead. Overhead includes everything from paying for the electricity to run the computer to the cost of insurance. Business owners pay for accounting/tax/bookkeeping help, telephone services, website maintenance, and any benefits they would have been getting from their jobs. A percentage of the overhead needs to be considered as part of pricing.

Bulk Pricing

Your price may go up or down based on how much is being purchased. For instance, many consultants give discounts to clients that purchase services on a monthly retainer model, because there is a set amount of work that will be coming in. Software providers often give discounts for longer contracts. Consider whether to price based on longer or greater commitments.

What the Market Will Bear

If the market will bear a higher price, you should usually charge it. Be aware that you always need to be competitive, but if you've got a stellar reputation or are offering something truly unique, people will pay a premium for that uniqueness.

From Joe: A Warning

Joe has a lot to say about pricing, as he is an antitrust expert. He wants you to know the following:

Why not just call up others who are doing what you want to do and ask what they charge? That way you can find out if there is a consensus on how to charge. If this sounds smart, then you did not pay attention in the antitrust training session. Discussions among competitors about pricing, which clients to pursue, and what prices to charge on bids put you on the road to damnation.

The Sherman Act in the US, and similar laws all around the world, bar agreements and understandings between competitors about competitive matters. While it might just seem to you that you are innocently gathering information, you may be inviting criminal charges of price-fixing, bid rigging, and market allocation. Do not call your competitors to discuss such matters related to competition. And if you think someone doing consulting in this field is not really a "competitor," the odds are dangerously high that you are wrong. This is a global market. You could easily be a competitor, no matter what the location of the other provider. This is dangerous territory, so as you have told your own clients, know the rules first.

Also, do not be lulled into a false sense of security that this is something everyone has been doing for years, so it must be ok. This is, sadly, a common phenomenon regarding white-collar crime. Edgy conduct seems acceptable until it suddenly is not. In such an environment it then becomes easy for the government to track down offenders and prosecute them. And at least one study has shown that the worst possible defense to use in front of a jury when it comes to white-collar crime is that "everybody else was doing it."

There are legitimate sources of pricing information. Neutral studies and surveys are one source. You can also talk with customers. But avoid anything that looks like you are coordinating with competitors.

Bottom line:

- Do not discuss prices with your competitors or agree in any way with competitors on pricing.
- Do not call your competitors to find out "what the right price range is" or anything else like that. This is price-fixing.
- Don't agree with competitors on markets, such as dividing up areas or types of customers or types of services. Agreeing that you will handle one city and they will handle another, or you will handle one type of company and they will cover another, is what is called market allocation and is illegal.
- Don't agree on bids. Do not discuss who will get this bid and who gets the next. Don't agree to submit a fake bid so someone else can win. This is called bid rigging.
- Do not use this section of this book as legal advice. Go to counsel if you have questions.

Now That You've Started...Is It Working?

Steve Blank is a serial Silicon Valley entrepreneur who has created, built, and sold a number of businesses.

After selling his eighth business, Blank started to articulate an idea he calls "The Lean Start-Up."

As he tells the story, he asked himself, "Why have I succeeded in launching businesses when so many have failed?" And, for Blank, the answer lay in one key insight, plus a concept he calls "customer development."

Blank's key insight is this: A start-up is not yet a known business. Instead, it's an experiment in search of a repeatable and scalable business model.

This can seem scary, but it is also incredibly liberating.

Your business is an experiment! That means you don't have to be attached to what you're doing or to the details in your business plan. Instead, know that everything you're doing is a hypothesis, from your central business idea to your marketing plan.

> *A start-up is not yet a known business. Instead, it's an experiment in search of a repeatable and scalable business model.*

Reimagine your process like this: You're trying something to see if it works. You're making well-informed guesses and then testing those guesses. It's possible to be wrong at first and still succeed! You can try things, pay careful attention to what works, and then adjust, tinkering with everything from the big picture to the details until you get it right.

Kirsten used this testing mindset for everything from Rethink's major lines of business to its marketing channels. When a marketing channel worked (one group's webinar brought in 117 attendees and multiple sales leads), she did more webinars with that group. When it didn't (another group's webinar had six people), she dropped it and didn't try it again.

"For me, a "testing" attitude allowed for a certain lightness of spirit," Kirsten said. "When something worked, it was a successful experiment. And when something didn't work, it was *also* a successful experiment. Either way, I knew more about what the market wanted from the business than I did before."

Once you embrace the concept of your business being an experiment, the second step is to practice what Blank calls "customer development."

This means you don't sit alone in a room and write a business plan based on a bright idea. Instead, you come up with ideas and then get out into the market and run them by your potential clients. And you do this in a spirit of inquiry; listening more than selling, being willing to be wrong.

If the feedback tells you that you're wrong, you tinker. You keep working on your product or service and keep getting feedback from potential buyers until someone demands to buy what you're selling. When a couple of clients do this, you know you have a viable business on your hands.

Assess and Adjust Until You Succeed

Not sure if you've got your market and product strategy right? The market will tell you.

It's simple, straightforward, and a tiny bit terrifying. In Steve Blank's model, only one metric matters: sales.

Sales indicate perceived value. If you're making sales, you've got your market validation. People want to buy what you're selling — hurray! If you're selling enough to pay your bills and pay yourself, you've got a business. As Google CEO Eric Schmidt says, "Revenue solves all known problems." Now, if you want to, you can concentrate on growing.

But what about when things are less clear?

Maybe you're having lots of conversations, getting lots of buzz, seeing lots of activity … but you're not closing business yet?

If you've been doing this for a while with slow or no sales, then you have your market feedback – and it's that you need to change something. Buzz and activity are great, but they can fool you.

If it doesn't eventually lead to sales, you're not where you need to be yet. Talk to your potential buyers, keep tinkering with your offer, and continue doing this until you start to see sales come in the door.

Keeping the Clients You Have

For nearly every business, it takes effort, time, attention, and money to attract and sign clients. So, if at all possible, take action to keep the clients you have!

This won't work for companies offering something that clients will buy only once. (Though...is there anything else you can sell them once you're done?)

But any company that has an opportunity for repeat business with the same clients should make it a priority to continue to "sell" to its existing customer base.

Sometimes, "sales" can be as easy as building a great relationship and delivering a great result for the first sale. When this happens, clients may proactively ask about other opportunities.

Other times, you may need to work a little for the sale. Maybe the client doesn't know you have other services to offer. Maybe you've added products or services they don't know about, so reach out to tell them.

As a company gets bigger and busier, this kind of work can sometimes fall by the wayside when the focus is on meeting day-to-day deadlines. Studies show that it takes five times more resources to attract new leads than to nurture the clients you already have, so treat those current and former clients like gold.

Taking the time to "sell" into your existing client base (something that can include asking for warm referrals to people they know) almost always will get you more hits than talking to strangers for the first time.

Now that the business is up and running, it's time to make sure everyone knows about it. That's where marketing, and our next section, comes in.

SECTION THREE: Marketing

You may have the greatest product or service in the world, but if no one knows about it, you won't make sales or be in business very long. Being able to market well is a critical skill. In this section we will dive deep into four important ways to market: writing, speaking, building an online presence, and networking.

CHAPTER 10

Writing

Kirsten loves to quote David Maister's *Managing the Professional Service Firm*:[5]

"Marketing works when it demonstrates, not when it asserts. Marketing tactics that illustrate one's competence (such as speeches, seminars, articles) are infinitely more powerful than those which assert it (such as brochures, direct mail, and 'cold calls' to 'let me tell you more about our firm')."

There's nothing as enduring as the written word to show your knowledge and to promote your skills in a subtle (or not so subtle) way while engaging your audience.

Compliance and ethics is a field where the ability to write is vital. Compliance program steps, such as writing policies, creating codes of conduct, developing effective communications tools, and communicating online, require written products. When managing a compliance program, writing like a lawyer is a prescription for failure. Communications need to be clearly understandable and have an impact. Writing can also be a powerful tool in building your professional reputation and developing a network.

Writing is effective because, done properly, it accomplishes a number of things. Writing can:

- Immediately notify potential clients that you understand the subject area in which they need help.
- Be used as support when you're pitching a potential client to show tangible expertise.

- Be timeless – writing can endure online or in book format forever.
- Help potential clients to find you if they Google your area of expertise.
- Expand your audience as people share your blogs or review your book(s).
- Help you to get speaking gigs that can expand your audience and reach potential clients in a new way.
- Create goodwill from potential clients who feel that you've already helped them to solve problems, even if you haven't met them yet.
- Introduce you to potential clients in a way that they feel they already know you when you reach out to talk to them.

Writing has been a critical marketing technique for Kirsten, Kristy, and Joe. Each has written countless pieces of thought leadership, whether in a book, e-book, blog, or other format. In this chapter, we'll explore how you can use writing to build and market your business for maximum impact.

What Should You Write About?

Writing to drum up business is different than writing while you're in-house without a plan to start a business. Researching, writing, and editing take time. The exact amount of time varies depending on the type of writing. Broadly speaking, you can create:

- a blog post
- an article for a magazine
- a magazine column
- a white paper
- an e-book
- a book
- a lengthy, substantive article

No matter the format, there are three broad categories of topics practitioners write about. These include:

Writing to the News

One common approach in writing for public consumption is to jump on recent headlines/developments and offer advice and commentary. This can draw press attention and garner significant publicity. It can, however, leave you hopping from topic to topic as each new story develops, which limits your ability to show a depth of expertise in one area.

The latest news tends to lend itself to shorter format writing such as blog posts. Without a doubt, it is easier to write a blog post than it is a lengthy, substantive article or book. Blog posts are typically 400 – 1,200 words. They can be written, edited, and posted within a day. If you're writing about a new case/prosecution, new regulatory guidance, or new law, it may be useful to get your opinion piece out as quickly as possible, as people will be hungry for information about the latest news event immediately but will tire of the deluge of opinions within a week.

Writing to Your Key Topic(s)

An alternative approach to commenting on headlines is to capture a niche and occupy that area as fully as possible. Your business objective could be to become the "go-to" person for that particular topic.

Kirsten, Kristy, and Joe have all used this strategy to grow their businesses. Rethink Compliance has maintained a blog since 2016. In fact, one of Kirsten's earliest hires was a part-time marketing person to help her generate and post content. Over the years, the blog has featured everything from a four-part code of conduct rewrite series, to a spoken word anti-harassment video, to video interviews over Zoom with clients. Potential clients who learn about Rethink often find their way to the blog and read through it. It's a great way for prospective clients to test drive the company's point of view and personality before making contact.

Joe decided to write about the specialist area of using incentives in compliance programs. Joe wrote the first (and as of this publication, only) white paper on this topic because he saw it as an important area that was being largely ignored. Whenever there was a news story or issue related to incentives, Joe easily contacted the author and provided input, or commented when there were online postings. When the Securities and Exchange Commission (SEC) and the Department of Justice (DOJ) wrote their guidance document on FCPA compliance programs, Joe's paper was the source they cited in this discussion. This publicity helped Joe to win consulting clients.

Kristy blogs weekly, frequently touching on topics relating to Spark Compliance's core offerings. For instance, if she's writing on how to perform a risk assessment, in the middle of the blog she'll note what a client at Spark Compliance did to complete the assessment successfully (linking to Spark's website), then at the end of the blog add a paragraph in italics saying, "Want more information on a professional risk assessment? Contact me at ____." The blog post will lead people to think about Spark Compliance and Kristy when they think about obtaining a risk assessment.

With all that said, do not write a pitch for your business and expect it to be published anywhere other than in paid advertising or on your own site. The best writing gives to your audience first, creating a feeling of reciprocity and gratitude for the information you shared. Show them your expertise, gain their trust, and then pitch your product.

Academic/Legal Writing

If your approach is not "sound-bite" writing, but more substantive, there are still formal journals that publish in-depth pieces. In the legal field, for example, law schools have law reviews that provide a means to reach the legal community. These are run by law students and typically follow a rigorous process. All sources must be cited, and all citations must follow a detailed standard. The law students will review each citation to be sure it supports the text. However, as is true with much of writing, whether it is actually read, and whether it has an impact, typically depends on you. Law reviews publish but generally do not promote their material. They also do not pay.

There is now a relatively easy way to have a substantial paper made available globally for academics and others conducting serious research. This is done by posting it on the Social Science Research Network (SSRN) https://www.ssrn.com/index.cfm/en/. Everything on the SSRN is available for free, and membership is free. In addition, the SSRN tracks how often your piece is seen and downloaded. However, if you publish your paper elsewhere first, you need to be sure you have permission to post it on the SSRN, since a publisher may resist posting it for free. The SSRN is also a helpful research source when writing a substantive piece. Substantial materials can also be listed on academia.edu and Google Scholar (scholar.google.com), which makes them more visible to academics writing in the field.

Finding Your Voice

As you start to develop your writing, you'll want to develop your unique voice. "Voice" refers to the style, structure, and vocabulary you choose. The most successful authors have an individualized voice. Whether it is Steven King's capacity to evoke the macabre in Maine, or Dan Brown creating excitement using historical facts mixed with conspiracy theories and imminent harm, writers draw in audiences with their unique way of sharing their stories. This is true with fiction and non-fiction. When you find an author with whom you resonate, you are likely to start reading and keep reading.

Early on, Kristy decided to adopt a friendly, relaxed, to-the-point style. "I wanted my writing to be accessible and non-academic, despite being an adjunct law professor at the time I started my blog. I also decided to be the queen of 'top tips' and 'to-do lists' to help make compliance officers' jobs easier. It has built me a following of like-minded people. Some people hate my style and find it shallow, and that's OK. I'd rather build a smaller audience of people who strongly relate to my writing style than a broader one that can't distinguish me from everyone else. I'm much more likely to be aligned with, and therefore sell to, people who like my style."

One distinctive and very different voice in compliance belongs to Broadcat founder Ricardo Pellafone. His company's blog often features cartoon cats or titles like "Using graphics to spark compliance email joy." Ricardo's (and, by extension, his company's) voice is intentionally edgy, provocative, slyly funny, and pop-culture savvy.

In a world of content, distinctive voices stand out. Just make sure to distinguish yourself in line with the way you want to present yourself and your company.

Should You Co-Author?

If you are a solo author, you have the advantage of not having to depend on someone else and having complete editorial control. If the writing is good, you also get all the credit. You can

ensure that everything in the piece is agreeable to you. But, as with other aspects of this field, it is not the only method. Finding a good partner or partners for your work can be both more efficient and more enjoyable.

One quick route to having a book published can be partnering with an established author and expert. This can open doors with publishers and editors, because the established author is a known supplier of good material, and the publisher or editor does not have to worry about getting publishable materials.

It is generally not advisable, however, just to be a prominent author's assistant, who merely gets mentioned in a footnote. These helpers are rarely, if ever, recognized otherwise, and the footnote reference provides no visibility. Footnote references should be for those who provide encouragement, check citations, or read a draft and provide comments. This should not be the fate of someone who has, in fact, been a co-author. Depending on the ego of the main author, you may be quickly forgotten, notwithstanding that you have done the bulk of the work. If you are going to partner with another writer, be sure you share the byline and aren't placed in a footnote.

If you co-author a major work with a well-known author, you can then follow up by writing pieces that build on, and help publicize, the book. Many authors forget that books do not sell themselves. As a co-author, you can extract useful points from the book and publish shorter pieces based on those materials.

One way you can employ this technique is to create a numbered list from your book's material. So if the book is about training, a co-author could develop an interesting article drawing 10 tips on effective training from the book. Depending on the inclinations of the co-author, this could be either a joint or solo project. But it has the dual benefit of promoting the book, plus giving you a wider reach.

The Power of Going Against the Grain

Alan Weiss is a godfather of consulting. He's written books like *Million Dollar Consulting* and *The Consulting Bible*. He attributes much of his success to his self-described "contrarian" style. He likes to go against the crowd, arguing against popular ideas within the business community to stand out. Looking at Mr. Weiss' body of work, there's no denying that being a contrarian has worked for him.

The contrarian approach can be highly successful in the compliance field. Choosing an unpopular or novel opinion and writing about it can bring attention quickly.

Kristy used this strategy early on. In January 2016, when Spark Compliance was about to launch, the ISO 37001 anti-bribery management standard was a hot topic. It was to be published later that year and was novel for the compliance field in that it was a certification standard, meaning that companies meeting the standard's requirements could be certified for having an effective anti-bribery program.

Kristy read the standard and thought it was extremely useful. She could see that nearly all of the commentary in the compliance world was against the ISO standard, so she decided to be a voice in favor. She wrote a piece for the FCPA blog that, by compliance standards, immediately went viral. Soon, thought leaders like Alexandra Wrage. Tom Fox, and Hui Chen were responding with their own articles and blog posts pushing back at Kristy's opinions, frequently referring to her directly. This created a perception that she was on a similar playing field as the icons who had been around for years. It created a buzz in the profession, amplifying Kristy's voice.

Joe often made a point of challenging the accepted wisdom or common approaches. For instance, in years past, small companies complained that they could not afford compliance programs, unlike the huge companies like those listed on the New York Stock Exchange (NYSE). Joe saw this as nonsense, as he had decades of experience dealing with small businesses. In his view, the problem wasn't that compliance programs were expensive; it was that entrepreneurs wanted to avoid dealing with legal details so they could focus exclusively on the business side of things.

So Joe wrote the SCCE white paper, "A Compliance & Ethics Program on a Dollar a Day: How Small Companies Can Have Effective Programs."[6] This paper followed all the elements of the Sentencing Guidelines and showed how compliance steps could be implemented spending very little extra money (literally, with $365). This prompted invitations to speak internationally on the issue of compliance programs for small businesses and was used by the Department of Commerce internationally. It helped provide pushback to those who resisted having government credit compliance programs because that would be "unfair" to small businesses.

Finding a Unique Topic

The other way to stand out is to choose a topic or angle that hasn't been popular or covered at length, then make your name using that point of view. Perhaps you can be the person who writes intelligently about how new technologies can be used to kickstart compliance? Perhaps you can dive deep into behavioral economics, with techniques for applying it consistently within compliance programs?

Do people already write about technology and behavioral economics? Yes, but not consistently enough or with enough depth to make them known for those topics in the compliance world. Choose something different and differentiate yourself by making it "your thing."

The Importance of Editing

Errors in writing can undermine your credibility, and even make work look amateurish. It is worthwhile to find someone who can perform the editing function, such as a mentor (for lawyers, any former law review editor), or someone who teaches English or writing. There are also professional editors who can be found online, such as on Reedsy.com.

You should not rely on spellcheck for editing. It does not catch all errors, can actually create errors, and does not do fact-checking. Writing is an area where humility is a value. Those reviewing your piece can help you avoid mistakes and improve your final product.

If you're writing a book, you'll want to use a style guide to help you make it look professional. In the United States, the Chicago Manual of Style is the gold standard for this activity. It includes standards for grammar, capitalization, and other elements that will raise your book to the standard expected by readers.

Writing to Network

Once you've begun your writing, you can use it to network. There are two primary ways to do this: collaboration and sharing.

Collaboration

Joe is the king of using collaboration for networking and business development. When Joe writes an article, blog post, or book, he likes to circulate it to his confidants and others within the compliance community to get their feedback and ideas. In doing so, two important things happen. First, Joe ends up with a better article because he has vetted it with the people who will be his audience. Second, people who have contributed to a piece feel a sense of ownership and are much more likely to highlight the piece to their friends, colleagues, and on their social media channels.

When you've written a piece that you're proud of, consider sharing it with a small audience before you publish it. Request feedback, comments, or contributions. You can use this technique to network with people you don't know well or at all. Simply send them the piece or ask if you can, noting that they are thought leaders in the field or have the exact experience you're looking for to be able to comment effectively. Everyone likes to be acknowledged as a skilled thought leader with important commentary to add.

Because collaborators have knowledge of the field, they may catch substantive errors and be aware of sources or points that are new to you. It is far better to have errors noticed and corrected before having a piece published online than having the first commentator publicly point out some egregious omission. That does not help one develop a good reputation.

Receiving Criticism

What do you do in the review process if someone dislikes your work, how you wrote it, or disagrees with your fundamental points? This is where your personal judgment and experience come in. Be humble and consider the other person's alternative. Try to see things from that person's perspective. Challenge and test out your own thesis. If, after openly considering the other person's point, you still believe in your point and are prepared to work at it, you may be the one who in fact establishes that your point is right and that others need to open their minds to change.

If the criticism relates to a small point or a drafting point, you might use a rule of two or three. If just one person shares a criticism, you decide on your own whether it is right. But if two or three people raise the same point, you may wish to reconsider. However, do not simply fold and walk away because someone who is a big name dislikes what you are saying.

Sharing Your Work with the World

Once you've written a great piece, be sure to share it. Put it up on all of your social media channels and ask close friends to do so as well. If it is a longer piece, like a white paper, e-book, or book, write blog posts highlighting ideas within the book so that you can get word out of the larger piece more easily.

Kristy likes to create tools or write white papers, which she then shares via email with clients and prospective clients. "We have our white papers professionally laid out and designed. Once I'm satisfied that it is top-notch, I challenge myself to send out at least 100 copies via individual emails to our current, past, and prospective clients. I've learned that sending something of value creates a much higher response rate than simply sending advertising or 'let's catch-up' emails."

Should You Write a Book?

One of the questions we're asked most often is whether or not a person should write a book. Writing a book is a monumental undertaking and shouldn't be committed to lightly. There are definitely pros and cons to writing a book.

The Pros

Writing a book cements you as an expert in a way that nothing else can. When a person is shown on television, more often than not the expert is credited as the "author of the book _____." Being an author who has written on a topic literally makes you the person who "wrote the book" on the subject. This comes with instant credibility and can make a big difference to your trajectory.

Writing a book can lead to invitations for speaking engagements which can broaden your audience. It can also lead to articles being written about you, and interviews and podcasts highlighting your book. Free publicity is one of the best reasons to write a book.

If your book is good, people will share it and buy it for each other. For instance, many compliance teams read *How to Be a Wildly Effective Compliance Officer* so they can discuss how to apply it to the business in which they operate. This engagement has enhanced Kristy's reputation and won her fans that she wouldn't have had the ability to reach otherwise.

The Cons

Writing a book is a gargantuan effort. For most people, the writing process is arduous and can take months, if not years. There is always the possibility that people won't like your book; or worse, that no one will buy it or read it at all.

It will likely take a large amount of your time trying to find a publisher, if you can find one at all. If you self-publish, you'll need to hire graphic designers, interior layout artists (or purchase software to do so), and cover designers to help you to create a credible offering, which can cost thousands of dollars. Many people simply don't have the discipline, focus, or ideas to create a book.

Think long and hard before you commit to writing a book. If you get it right, it can be a huge win. If you don't, it can be a long, embarrassing time-suck with little to show for your effort and money.

Making Money with Writing

Can you make money from your writing? Yes, you can. Royalties from books are the obvious way to make money as an author. However, you probably shouldn't start buying cars too quickly with your anticipated windfall when your book is done. With major publishers, book royalties can be as small as 10% of the purchase price. Worse still, many non-profits publish books with no royalties whatsoever going to the author. Are those books worth writing? Sure – if you're writing for reach and publicity and not for cash.

At the same time, small royalties can build up to relatively big money over time. For instance, *How to Be a Wildly Effective Compliance Officer* has sold well over 10,000 copies, and it continues to sell an average of 100 to 200-plus books per month. The sales of that book have created fans who have bought Kristy's later books and online courses, creating an even larger income stream.

Writing a book can also lead to speaking gigs, some of which can be quite lucrative. Notable speakers in the field regularly earn thousands of dollars per keynote. This isn't true for most speakers in compliance; but for a select few, it provides a lucrative living.

Once you've written a successful book, technology companies and magazines in the compliance field frequently offer you money to write and promote articles. The going rate is usually between $500 and $2,500 per article.

If you are a lawyer and enjoy writing, law books can earn you thousands of dollars a year. They may also have annual supplements. These increase the revenue potential of the book but can involve substantial amounts of research and work. Although, there is professional value in having to update one's knowledge about the field and to keep up with recent developments.

You can make money writing for the compliance field. However, none of us recommend trying to do so on a full-time basis. Writing can be a nice supplement to consulting and other business activities, but it is unlikely to sustain you by itself.

Our Experiences

"Writing *How to Be a Wildly Effective Compliance Officer* was the best thing I ever did for my business," said Kristy. "It gave me a platform and a voice. It led to speaking gigs all over the world. It led to my first appearance in the *Wall Street Journal*, to my monthly magazine column that's about to enter its sixth year, and to my cover story in *Compliance and Ethics Professional Magazine*. It gave me credibility and fans in a way nothing else could."

For Joe, writing was part of his beginning in the compliance field. Joe has published articles, books, book chapters, and white papers, and even started what was probably the first compliance newsletter in 1991 (*Corporate Conduct Quarterly*, subsequently merged into *Ethikos*). His white paper on incentives, for example, was cited as an authority in the DOJ and SEC guide on the FCPA. His first article on the self-evaluative privilege was cited by a federal district court and a state supreme court.

"Writing was my vehicle into public speaking, networking, interaction with governments, and generating business," Joe said. "All of this helped establish my identity in compliance and ethics that helped each business I was involved in to attract clients."

Kirsten notes, "In 2019, the SCCE published my book *Creating Great Compliance Training in a Digital World.*[7] In a crazy stroke of luck, it came out the same month that Rethink introduced our compliance training library. All our advertising that year said, 'We wrote the book on compliance training' – a great tagline! The book buzz created a lot of opportunities. I was on podcasts. I was featured on the cover of *Compliance and Ethics Professional Magazine*. There was a giant poster of me at an industry conference where I had a book signing. It gave the company a boost, put our compliance library in the spotlight, and changed my career forever."

The "How-to" of Writing

If you have an idea you want to develop, how do you convert this into a publishable piece? One way is to use a five-step process: 1) develop ideas; 2) draft the outline; 3) write the draft 4) review and edit; and 5) publish.

Step One: Develop Ideas

Step one is developing ideas. At the ideas stage, you (and any co-author) develop ideas and write them down. This form of brainstorming can go on for quite some time until you are satisfied that you have captured what you want to cover. In this process, you may be doing research, finding helpful quotes, and even writing things that will ultimately be grafted into the final text.

Step Two: Outline

Step two is creating the outline. Here you organize the points in a way that makes sense to you and that flows. It is useful to begin with something that will catch the reader's attention. In the beginning, you tell the reader what you are going to cover. For a lengthy piece, there is value in starting with a list of key points that will be covered in the paper. You can also plan to include helpful lists or tools if the book is intended as a guide for practitioners.

Step Three: Draft

The third step is the drafting. If the outline is done well, this can be a fairly straightforward process. It is a bit like adding hot water to an instant beverage – you are just adding words to the ideas that are already spelled out in the outline.

Step Four: Review and Edit

The fourth step is reviewing and editing the manuscript. Usually, the author begins with their own review of the preliminary product. While one author may be ready to send this early product out to others for review, another might find that they end up re-writing, re-organizing, and re-doing most of it. The end product may be very different from the first draft.

"I've written numerous books, and with each of them, I inevitably end up re-ordering much of the book, rewriting certain sections, and combining others. The review process is, for me, the most creative and challenging. Editing is hard, but it makes the end product significantly better than the first draft," said Kristy.

When the self-review is done, the next step is to entice others to read and comment on the piece.

Step Five: Publish

Once you've completed the review, it's time to publish or submit the piece to publishers.

The bad news is that compliance is still a niche field, so there are fewer places to publish than, say, in the health and wellness niche. The good news is that a consolidated number of outlets means that it is relatively easy to reach a wide audience of potential clients.

Where can you publish? Consider:

- your own website or blog
- a personal compliance-related blog run by an industry expert

- blogs published by non-profit organizations in the compliance field
- technology vendors that maintain a blog
- LinkedIn
- traditional book publishers
- vanity book publishers (companies you pay to write and/or publish a book in your name for your personal distribution)
- specialist book publishers
- law reviews/journals
- compliance-related magazines
- magazines aimed at boards of directors or other executives
- business-related blogs (e.g., Forbes, Fortune, Inc.)
- university publications or presses
- via technology vendors' platforms
- via e-book housed on your website
- via Amazon

Once you've made your list of potential publications and publishers, collate their information into a spreadsheet. Your spreadsheet should list the name of the publisher/publication, contact information for submission, and any other important notes. Follow the writers and/or editors on LinkedIn and Twitter, then highlight, post, tweet, and re-tweet their content so they start to know your name. By doing this, you'll begin to create a relationship. When you contact them about publishing your work, they'll know who you are, which will make it much easier to get published.

Read the Fine Print

Many publishers put out publication guidelines. Before you begin writing, research the publication guidelines at the place(s) you've highlighted for your work. Many publications have word limits (e.g., blogs must be between 400 and 1,200 words), or request a certain style (e.g., formal, like a law journal; or informal for blog posts). You don't want to get halfway through your article before you realize that it won't be considered in the venue for which you're writing.

Just Write Something...Then Keep Writing

Whether you write a magnum opus on compliance or a simple 400-word blog post, start writing. Writing gives you credibility. It gives you something to hand out to potential clients. It shows your knowledge in a way that talking about your knowledge never could. Start writing once a week, and keep to your schedule. Writing is the secret sauce to the success of so many businesses in the compliance field. Make sure yours is one of them.

CHAPTER 11

Public Speaking

According to numerous surveys, the majority of people fear public speaking more than they fear death. If you are one of them, it's time to get over your fear, as public speaking is one of the best ways to advertise your business and to prove your expertise.

Author Brian Tracy said, "Communication is a skill that you can learn. It's like riding a bike or typing. If you're willing to work at it, you can rapidly improve the quality of every part of your life." Public speaking can be scary. After all, you're putting yourself in front of a group of people who will inevitably judge you. Regardless, it's worth it to get out on the stage to support your business. And this is definitely a skill that you can learn by study and practice.

One useful tip to consider before you do any speaking is this: Audiences routinely have a higher opinion of a speaker if someone else introduces the speaker. So wherever you speak, find a way for someone – anyone, really – to introduce you, rather than introducing yourself.

The Benefits of Public Speaking

The value of public speaking cannot be overstated. Public speaking creates numerous benefits. These include the following:

Showing, Not Telling Your Expertise

As with writing, it is vastly preferable to *show* your expertise to potential clients than to simply *tell* them you have it.

A good presentation full of useful information immediately benefits your potential client, making them much more inclined to hire you – after all, you've already helped them.

For example, in one SCCE Institute, Joe gave a talk on a topic connected with his book, *501 Ideas For Your Compliance and Ethics Program*.[8] As a result of tying the book to the topic, he had an attendee order 100 copies for her compliance colleagues and retained Joe to do work for the company.

And that's just one of many examples. Joe also recalls giving a talk at a Practising Law Institute program early in his consulting career where he finished the conference with three new corporate clients. While people often already knew about him because of his long-term activities in the field, there was no question that the presentations triggered the decision to retain his firm.

People Keep Material with Your Company Name on It

In many venues, you will be allowed to hand out worksheets, white papers, and supplemental materials that attendees can take home with them.

Assuming that the material is relevant to their jobs (and it should be – you don't just want a brochure that will be thrown away), the potential client is likely to keep it and occasionally refer to it. If the potential client pulls out your material a year later, they will be reminded of you and your capacity to help them. That white paper may win you a major contract.

For example, some time ago, Kristy created a white paper titled "Choosing Metrics that Matter" that included more than 60 example metrics. She brought 400 to a session she was running, and they were all taken before the session ended.

Nine months later, she was contacted by a person who had attended the session to see if Spark Compliance could perform a compliance program review. "The chief compliance officer specifically mentioned that she'd kept the white paper and referred to it frequently. I'm sure that's what gave us the edge to win the contract."

You'll Be More Likely to Be Asked to Speak Again

If you do a good job, the people who see you speak will likely recommend you to other conference producers, or they may ask you to speak on a panel or be a co-speaker with you at another event. Success begets success, and speaking successfully at one event is likely to get you invited to others.

The fact that you were selected to present conveys the message that you are a reliable and safe speaker. Those putting together another program know they can slot you in as a sure thing.

You'll Hone Your Skills with Each Presentation

Each speaking session is a chance to improve your presentation skills. Even if one session isn't stellar, by reading the comments and considering where you could have been more effective, you'll naturally improve.

People Can See Your Personality

Not every potential client will be a match for you and your style. Some in-house practitioners prefer to work with staid lawyers, where others prefer large personalities and someone they can imagine having a drink with after a long day of interviews.

"Our style is based on my in-house experience, so I tend to be very pragmatic and to boil things down to their basics. This is the opposite of many of the big law and accounting firms. When someone sees me speak, they can tell how I will approach their project. If they like me, then we're a match," said Kristy.

Being a match is important because winning a project with a client that has a totally different style and expectations can lead to frustration on both sides. If a potential client sees your personality and likes it, that can get you halfway to a paying project.

You Can Showcase Your Offerings (Subtly)

When you're on stage, you're going to give examples and tell stories from your life and work. Many of your stories will naturally begin with, "We were working with a client on a situation like this..." When you give advice and best practices in the context of your work with your clients, you'll be able to subtly tell people what you do without broadcasting your services like a television commercial.

A Caveat

Be aware that, as a vendor, there may be a bias against having you speak for fear that you will just give a sales presentation.

Whenever possible, Kirsten arranges to co-present with in-house practitioners, whether clients or contacts. Some conferences prefer to have in-house people speaking, so this pairing can open doors. Also, the client can say positive things about your firm that are more credible than anything you might say about yourself. Finally, talking about actual projects keeps the focus of the talk squarely on practical applications – which is more valuable to the practitioners in the audience.

When it's not possible to co-present, Kirsten tries to include case studies and anecdotes in place of the practitioner's presentation, where she can share some details about actual projects. (There are ways to do this without revealing the client's name or anything confidential about their situation.)

Either way, the goal is to talk through your thoughts and ideas in the context of a real-life situation. This lets you naturally and convincingly demonstrate that you understand the situation, you understand a typical client's needs and goals, and you can support them in bringing exactly this kind of project to a successful conclusion.

While You're In-House

When you're in-house, the phone may ring frequently with invitations to speak at conferences and events. If you're senior in your role or known as a good speaker, you may get calls on a near-weekly basis. If you're on the speaking circuit when you leave the in-house world to start your business, it may come as a shock when those speaking requests dry up, with many conference producers requiring payment to allow you to speak. In fact, some conferences charge upwards of $25,000 for a speaking slot (none of us has done that, but we've been solicited).

This is not the case with presenters like Practising Law Institute and the SCCE, but they still seek to have speakers who are in-house when possible. Because of this, Kirsten, Kristy, and Joe recommend taking every speaking opportunity you can while you're still in-house to develop your skill and to spread awareness of your expertise.

The best-case scenario is to be known as a good speaker before you leave the in-house world. If you can, choose a specialty that is related to your ambitions for your company. For instance, if you know you'll be starting a training company, begin speaking about best practices in training while you are still in-house.

At Integrity Interactive, one person developed expertise in third-party management and quickly became the go-to speaker on that topic. He subsequently reversed the process, going from the vendor world to working in-house. His strategy clearly worked. In this way, you will be able to develop a reputation for your area of specialization.

It isn't just conference speaking that can be cultivated while you're in-house. Being in-house can present frequent opportunities to speak publicly as part of your compliance program training and in presentations for management. This is an excellent opportunity to practice.

Getting Started

If you're nervous about starting, there are lots of great speaking coaches and workshops available, both live and online. Early in her career, Kirsten took a helpful course from Dale Carnegie Training. Then in 2015, just before starting Rethink Compliance, she took a two-day speaking workshop from a company called Own The Room. There, she learned a range of things, from mindsets (forget about yourself and focus on the audience) to tactics (give people one takeaway), many of them powerfully effective. The workshop-style event gave her a chance to see her fellow students put these strategies into action, and many of them improved substantially in less than 24 hours.

As part of the training, she was videotaped giving a two-minute, impromptu talk – and was surprised to see that she was already a better speaker than she thought she was. This gave her the confidence to pursue more speaking opportunities as she worked to grow the company.

There are specific techniques for reducing anxiety (e.g., visit the speaking site beforehand and stand at the podium when no one is there, using dramatic pauses, and making eye contact) that can all be developed while speaking in-house. When you're starting, it is worth researching public speaking and even hiring a coach to help you improve.

Where to Speak

There are many venues in which to speak. Each has its pros and cons.

In-Person Conferences

The most obvious place to speak is conferences. Conferences are great because you spend a significant amount of time with the other attendees. Before your session, you can talk about it with others, giving you an easy conversation starter. After your speech, people may be inclined to talk to you because they feel like they've gotten to know you a bit, and they can relate their own experiences or ask questions related to your topic.

On the con side, your experience at conferences can shift dramatically when you move from in-house speaker to vendor. Kristy hadn't expected this, and it was painful. "I went from being someone that everyone wanted to talk to and court to being someone many people avoided because the word 'consultant' was on my nametag. People don't want to be sold to, so they may avoid anyone who isn't in-house. It was a difficult realization to find out I was suddenly on the outside."

Nevertheless, you should target conferences as they usually have the greatest concentration of potential clients of any speaking format. Think broadly about conference producers. There are large national conferences, as well as regional and local ones. Non-profit organizations hold conferences, as do compliance-related, for-profit organizations. Many of the vendors in the technical space hold conferences, so be sure to reach out to them to see if you can speak at their events.

Getting a speaking slot at these conferences can be competitive, so it is important to have a topic that is likely to appeal to the conference's audience. As noted, teaming with someone in-house can help in this process. Practical, how-to presentations are particularly useful for attendees. It can also give you a competitive edge if the conference organizers already know you, as is likely if you've published good written material in their publications.

Another trick of the trade is that, as is true in writing, offering numbered lists has a particular appeal. A proposed talk called "15 Tips for Effective Training" may have more appeal than one called simply "Effective Training."

Webinars and Online Conferences

Webinars and online conferences have become more popular than ever. Since COVID-19 hit in 2020, more and more events have moved online. The technology for holding webinars and online conferences has been advancing significantly, and the ease of staying at a desk instead of having to travel has made these activities a popular draw.

Webinars and online conference presentations have the obvious benefit of saving the time and expense of traveling to a conference. When you are in-house, if you are a conference speaker, many organizations will pay for your travel expenses, as well as conference entrance fees. (For professionals, this has the advantage of getting continuing education credits for free.) This is almost never true for travel expenses when you're a vendor, so the opportunity to present without travel costs is definitely a plus. Webinars and online conferences also have the benefit of reaching a large, and potentially global, audience instead of a more local or regional event.

As with all speaking, it pays to choose topics that relate to your company's work. Kristy loves giving webinars about topics that relate to Spark's offerings. "Risk assessments are one of our most popular products. I've done at least 10 webinars focusing on risk assessment methodology. Some have been panels, others have been solo or with a co-presenter; but in each one, I've been able to share information about how we do risk assessments and how we work with clients. It's definitely won us business because we were able to show our expertise without shouting about it."

However, webinars and online conferences present their own difficulties. First, the lack of capacity to obtain real-time feedback can be unnerving. Some platforms allow the speaker to see some members of the audience, but if the audience is large or has its cameras turned off, you may feel like you're speaking to the void. While the audience can see your personality online, it's not the same as being there in person, where you can use your voice and body to convey ideas more powerfully. You're also much less likely to have people come up to you afterward with questions or to have a quick chat than you would be at a traditional conference. However, if you are active on LinkedIn, you may get immediate feedback through that medium, even when people have seen or heard your presentation through another means.

Podcasts

Podcasts are fast becoming a medium of choice. There are several popular compliance-related podcasts, and we expect that more will launch in the future. Each podcast has a different angle, but with some thinking, you can almost certainly come up with a topic that will be of interest to the producer or host. Podcasts need guests and new material on a near-constant basis. If you can offer top tips or creative ideas that can be used by compliance practitioners, you can almost certainly get on to a podcast.

The benefit of podcasts is that most are evergreen. While some revolve around the news of the day and therefore become dated, most focus on topics that can be searched by listeners and found by new listeners looking through the back catalog.

The challenge with podcasts is that many in the compliance field do not let you directly promote your products or offering. Regardless, they can boost your status as an expert by presenting you as someone uniquely worth listening to.

Go Live

Many social media sites have the capacity to "go live," meaning that you schedule a time for your audience to interact with you in real time. You turn on your camera, push the button, and you are suddenly live for the world to see. Most go-lives are recorded so that people can access them after you've spoken.

The benefit of going live is that you can have direct interaction with your audience. People who have joined your session can comment, ask questions in real time, and interact with you. You can speak about important topics in an impromptu way, which may make you more relatable than when you perform in a structured conference setting.

Going live is still a relatively new concept in the compliance world. It may be difficult to get an audience for your go-live, especially as people tend to work throughout the day at the office, and then not want to get on to a work-related social media platform once they've stopped working for the day.

Videos and Online Classes

Another way to present yourself as a speaker is to film/offer videos and online classes. Videos on channels like YouTube allow you to speak directly to your audience in a way they can access virtually anywhere at any time. Online classes are growing in popularity and are likely to continue to do so.

Video and online classes are beneficial in that they are available throughout the world with little cost to you once they are produced. Additionally, online classes can be sold directly from the internet, which can create passive income. Lastly, when people take an online class from you or watch your videos, they begin to feel that they know you, which makes them much more likely to continue buying your products and services or to bring you in for a large project.

On the negative side, the compliance profession has yet to embrace video and online classes the way that other industries have. You may put a great deal of time and effort into something that few people see, which can be disheartening.

Going Pro: Getting Paid to Speak

In 2016, Kristy had been planning to use the debut of her book to launch her professional speaking career, but it still came as a shock when she got her first offer. "I was contacted by a conference producer who had seen me speaking at an unpaid conference. He asked me what my terms were, and I had no idea what to say. I asked him to pay for my airfare from London to the States, and to give me a hotel room. He seemed rather shocked that I hadn't asked for a speaking fee. He then asked me to send my speaker agreement. I said I would. I didn't have a speaker agreement, so I had to find one online. It was not a great start to my speaking career!"

Once again, this shows that you don't need to know everything before you start. You just need to start, and you can learn as you go. Now Kristy has a stock speaking engagement contract as well as standard terms. "I can fill the form out in about 10 minutes," she said.

Getting paid to speak can be a tremendous milestone. Instead of begging (or paying) for a slot to speak, conference producers and potential clients come directly to you. It can be tough transitioning from a lay speaker to a professional one, but if you're a talented speaker, it is definitely worthwhile.

How to Start

The first thing is to decide that you want to be a public speaker. There is a big difference between being a good lay speaker and crossing over into the professional world.

Once you've determined that you will be a professional, begin honing your message. What makes you special? What is your topic going to be? And, perhaps most pertinently, who is your audience? Being the world's best speaker on trade sanctions is highly unlikely to be a topic that people will pay for because they can contact their lawyer who will likely speak for free.

The topics that people tend to pay for in the compliance field include:

- Whistleblowers with true-life stories.
- Criminals/people who have gone to jail for compliance violations and have reformed.
- Soft skills applicable to compliance. These can include:
  - time management
  - persuasion, motivation, and influence
  - handling different types of personalities
  - leadership skills
  - handling different age groups/generational differences
  - creating trust
- People with a specialist background or area of research. These can include:
  - behavioral science
  - white-collar crime
  - criminology
- Ethics as it applies to business.
- The reasons people make ethical/unethical choices.

Your topic or area of expertise needs to be niche and defined. Simply saying that you're a speaker on compliance and ethics won't cut it. You need to give people a reason to bring you into their company or conference.

Creating a Sizzle Reel

Potential buyers will always want to see you perform before they decide to hire you. You need to have bite-sized videos of you performing, preferably with the audience responding with laughter and clapping. You can create this in one of two ways.

First, you can ask for permission to record your session when you are speaking. Many conferences will allow you to film if you ask. Ideally, bring in a professional crew to film. If that's not feasible, have someone you know film on a high-quality camera on a tripod.

The other way to get a good reel is to find or rent a room with a stage and bribe your friends with food or drinks to come listen to you speak while you film the session. If your friends will allow themselves to be filmed smiling, laughing, and paying attention, you can splice this footage into your reel, which makes it more powerful.

Once you've got your raw material, either get an editing program, or better yet, hire an editor to put your reel together. You can use simple clips, which you can add to YouTube or Vimeo. You must have footage of yourself performing, or no one will hire you.

Create a One-Sheet

In addition to your sizzle reel, you'll want to create a downloadable one sheet. A one sheet is a one- or two-page full-color advertisement showing your expertise and major topic. It should include:

- professional photos — one headshot and one showing all or most of your body
- the title(s) of your keynotes (no more than three)
- reviews/testimonials
- a list of media that has featured you

Your Speaker Page on Your Website

Your sizzle reel and your one sheet should live on your website, along with a "contact me" form. Be sure to allude to the fact that you charge for your speaking by writing something like, "contact me for dates and rates." Your one sheet should be downloadable.

You'll also want to create a media kit, which can be on a second page. Your media kit should include your short bio, long bio, and speaker introduction, along with high-resolution and web-sized photos that clients can download to use in their media.

Pricing and Contracts

One of the biggest challenges people face is deciding how much to charge. Your price will likely start small – perhaps $500 or $1,000. Speakers in the compliance field make up to $13,000 for a one-hour speech (as of the time of writing). An average rate for sought-after speakers in the industry is between $5,000 and $7,500. If you become successful, six-figure incomes from speaking are not unusual.

The downside of speaking is that it requires an inordinate amount of travel. People see the speaker fees and get wide-eyed, but if you have to fly transatlantic, you'll be burning two travel days plus at least one day at the conference. When you divide the rate by the number of hours you're traveling and away from home, the hourly rate goes down dramatically.

It is sometimes worthwhile to perform for free, even when you've established yourself as a pro. Kristy will speak without a fee only when the group is target-rich with an audience exclusively composed of compliance officers that could hire her. If she can gain a five or six-figure contract from someone in the audience, it is worth taking the time to perform *gratis*.

Creating Your Keynote

Non-professional speakers tend to think that they need to come up with a new keynote for each gig. That is the opposite of case in the professional world, where the best practice is to hone a single keynote (or two, max), and to become known for that keynote.

If you have written a book, the title of your keynote should mirror, or at least refer to, the book topic. This is because you'll want to sell your books at the events wherever possible or have the conference sponsor buy books at a discounted rate to give out as gifts to the attendees. Adding a book signing can be extremely lucrative, and attendees are more likely to keep your book if it's signed. "I've sold 1,600 books at a time to conference producers. It can more than double the fee they pay for my speaking," said Kristy.

How to Create Your Keynote

Many people jump into slide production instead of laying out their speech. A good practice is to write out the entire speech before doing anything else. You'll almost certainly need to move sections around. You may find you have far too much or far too little material, which means you need to edit. Be sure to include quotes, statistics, pictures, and activities that draw in the audience.

Once you've finalized the first draft of your speech, divide it into major sections with bullet points. Take those bullet points and make some slides with them, then find a professional slide designer and hand over the project. Unless you are a graphic designer, you want a professional to produce your slides. The audience will be able to tell the difference, and to be a professional, you have to use professionals.

Try to use pictures instead of words on your slides. You want the words to *trigger your stories* or help jog your memory as to what content comes next. Your slides are simply a tool when you're a pro. They can't be a crutch.

Practice your speech by reading the script along with the slides several times, then ditch the script and practice using only the slides as your guide. Professional speakers seldom use note cards and don't read from the page when they are in front of an audience.

Once your speech is complete, consider hiring a speaking coach to bring your presentation to life. Coaches can help you with cadence, pauses, and positioning on the stage. Their help can be invaluable in making the transition from amateur to pro.

Practice, Practice, Practice

Professional athletes practice nearly every day. If you want to be a professional speaker, you need to study the craft and practice regularly. You should be able to do your speech in your head at any time, even without the slides. This is one reason to practice a single keynote until it is perfect. The time you take to make it great will make you more salable.

Get Out There!

Whether professionally or not, get out there and speak. Mark Twain said, "There are only two types of speakers in the world. One, the nervous. Two, liars." It's worth overcoming your fear and nervousness to build your business. After you've begun speaking, your client base will expand, as will your reputation. When potential clients see you proving your worth and knowledge, they are more likely to consider you when they have an engagement. Moreover, your confidence will grow as you practice speaking, and that will attract clients as well.

Let's move from the world of speaking and writing to the virtual world of building your online presence.

CHAPTER 12

Building Your Online Presence

O nce upon a time, companies looking to establish a market presence made sure they were listed in the phone book (maybe even chose a name to land at the top of the list, like AAAA Plumbers) and took out ads in the newspaper. Some with more money and ambition would take out radio and even TV ads.

To actively promote their company, they hired a PR firm, which got them placement in newspaper and magazine stories. Or they put up billboards (as local stores and personal injury lawyers still do).

But today, like so much else in our digital world, many of the traditional marketing, networking, and promotional activities have moved online – along with your audience. If you want your company to register in your chosen market, mastering your online presence (and persona) can be a powerful tool.

The good news is that you can now reach your buyer directly – often for free (or very cheaply) and without going through intermediaries or gatekeepers.

You can make people aware of you, make yourself easy to find and contact, help them get to know you and what you offer, and even share material that will help drive leads through the door.

In this chapter, we'll talk about how to build your online presence. We'll also discuss the art of content marketing and how it can be applied in the compliance marketplace.

Getting Started: Website

As a starting point, you'll need:

- a website
- a company LinkedIn page
- a personal LinkedIn page

These don't have to be elaborate, especially to start – as they say in tech, "Shipped is better than perfect."

You can always improve on things as you go. Kirsten, for instance, created the first Rethink Compliance website in an afternoon in the summer of 2016.

She'd initially hoped to outsource the writing, but after a freelance marketer quoted her $3,000 for the work, she sat down with a website-building program, bought a domain name for $14.99, and had the first draft published to the web by dinnertime. (As of this writing, Strikingly, Wix, and Weebly are all good options if web design isn't your full-time job.)

That first website was a single scrolling page with about six sections — a banner title, The Case for Better Content, Our Team, Code Rewrites, Contact Us, and a blog.

All in, the page probably contained less than 1,500 words, but it proved remarkably durable — surviving more than four years as the company's primary landing page, with modest alterations. As of this writing, the Rethink website is finally undergoing a major upgrade, but it took a long time for the company to outgrow that early effort.

Kristy created her "Compliance Kristy" website while still in-house. She began blogging near the end of her tenure and added a page saying that she could be booked for professional speaking. Like Kirsten, Kristy's site took an afternoon to put up. She used the builder within the Weebly platform, which was free. A year later, Kristy hired a designer to update the Compliance Kristy website. By then it had a large amount of content, which needed professional categorization. That certainly wasn't true on day one.

So our best advice is: Get something up and then iterate as needed.

Our best advice: Get something up and then iterate as needed.

A few tips for creating a compelling website:

Make It Visually Attractive

Your website will be one of the first impressions that people have of your products, services, and brand.

We have become a very visual society. Design choices can communicate a lot about who you are, what your company is, and even who your ideal client might be. In fact, a recent study out of Stanford found that visual design and aesthetics mattered more than any other factor when consumers were evaluating a website to gauge a company's credibility.[9]

Colors, fonts, images, and layouts all set a tone. Think about what tone you want to strike and what kinds of visuals might align with your plans. Certain compliance businesses may want something formal, like that of a law firm. Others, particularly those in a creative field, might want a more modern look and feel, like that of a boutique ad agency.

Good news: The easiest-to-use website builders come with built-in themes. So, in many cases, you can simply review the library of templates, choose one that "feels" like your business and build your website from there.

Incidentally, one key step in creating a polished visual identity is to select and use a consistent set of colors – often one primary brand color plus one to three accent colors.

Colors can convey meaning and mood. It may be useful to review color theory to help you to subtly convey what your company stands for. Spark Compliance used this technique to help it to nonverbally communicate its style.

"We chose dark blue, which relates to calmness; grey, which is seen as stately and formal; and white, which relates to purity and ethics. We wanted potential customers to see us as a trustworthy, steady hand that could help them to get where they needed to go," said Kristy.

If you're building a business, you have many more important things to think about than color schemes, so a good option is to let professional designers do the work for you. Once you choose a website template with a built-in color scheme, adopt those same colors for the rest of your company materials.

Need a logo? Many designers offer those services online for very reasonable prices, from $5 options on Fiverr to freelancers working for hourly rates on Upwork and other gig marketplaces. Often, these sites feature extensive reviews that help you choose a talented, responsible freelancer.

Write for the Way People Read Online

It's important to get right to the point on your website. People online skim rather than read, so make it easy for them to quickly understand who you are and what your business offers.

Start with good content aesthetics: Make sure to choose fonts, font sizes, and colors that are easy to read, then write web-friendly content. Use headlines, section headers, bulleted lists, and short paragraphs. (You can find some great tips on a website called Copyblogger.)

Avoid writing large chunks of text as most online readers will simply skip over them. Here, it can help to follow the placeholder content in the website template you select. If there's a five-word headline, replace it with a five-word headline. If there's a short, two-sentence paragraph, replace it with content of the same length.

Typically, these templates have been optimized for online content. Professionally-created templates are typically maximized for readability on desktop, laptop, and mobile platforms. Text that doesn't look too long on a desktop may be nearly unreadable on a cell phone, so keep to the suggested length wherever possible.

Keeping to the placeholder content can be harder than it looks. This exercise will force you to boil down your background and offerings to short, pithy sentences – perfect for accommodating impatient online visitors.

Tell a compelling story

Sales trainers have a saying: Sell the sizzle, not the steak. This is based on the concept that people buy based on emotion then look for logic to justify their decisions.

"Your website isn't just a place to explain the products and services you offer – it's a place to sell yourself and the business," Kirsten said. "Don't just say what you offer – say why you offer it and why you're better positioned than anyone else to help your ideal client in this area. If you can, tell a good story about your business. What motivated you to offer these products and services? What problem are you passionate about solving?"

Most people will come to your website because they've heard about you or your company and are curious to learn more. In compliance especially, prospective buyers tend to gather lots of information before ever making contact.

Great website copy is your chance to sell before you even know you're selling or who you're selling to.

Need help coming up with your compelling story? Kirsten once took a seminar from executive coach Brendan Burchard, who coaches his audience to sum up their business using the following formula:

"I help x do y so they can z."

For example:

I help compliance programs make great online content so they can engage their learners and drive real culture change.

Or:

Our software helps companies to vet their third parties quickly so the business engages with compliance from the start.

The "so they can z" is the real magic here, because it gets you to what's really driving your potential buyers. They need "y" – why do they need it? What are their other options for it today? What are the downsides of the other "y"s on offer?

Answering these questions is how you help yourself stand out and convey confidence and passion in your offerings. Figure out your x, y, and z, and then build your website around that story.

Spark Compliance puts its unique selling point right up front in its tagline.

"We spent a long time coming up with our tagline, which is 'Pragmatic, proportionate, pro-business compliance and ethics solutions.' Since I was a chief compliance officer, one of our main selling points is that we provide solutions that are easily implemented and take into account business realities. From the minute a potential customer opens the Spark website, they see what makes us special," said Kristy.

Include a Call to Action

The very best websites and online interactions don't just present information – they allow you to take the next step.

The best online stores make it easy to buy.

The best online businesses make it easy to download a compelling e-book or article. In exchange, you provide your email – giving them a chance to send you more information and potentially draw you further into the sales cycle.

If you've ever subscribed to a five-day writing boot camp or downloaded a free breathing guide put out by a yoga teacher, you've participated in this process.

When it comes to your business website, think about the right call to action. What do you want someone to do after they've learned about you?

- Do you want to sell them something online?
- Do you want them to contact you for a no-strings-attached discussion about how you can help?

- Do you want them to sign up for something?
- Do you want their email address so you can continue marketing to them?

Whatever the call to action is, set up your website so it's easy for an interested person to take that action – ideally something that moves them one step closer to becoming a customer.

Getting Started: LinkedIn

LinkedIn is a fantastic tool for building and maintaining your professional networks. Also, if your desired reach is global, it is one of the easiest ways to reach an international audience. "I have contacts in places as distant as Bosnia and Paraguay who regularly respond to my LinkedIn posts," Joe said.

Unlike social media that people use in their personal time (Facebook, Twitter, Instagram), LinkedIn is mostly focused on work and work topics, so it offers you a way to connect to your audience in a professional context.

You'll want to create a company page on LinkedIn and also update your personal page to reflect your new business and position. Then, if you haven't already, get busy building your list of connections.

"For the first 15 years of my compliance career, I did very little with LinkedIn," Kirsten said. "I rarely connected to people, visited the page, or updated my profile. I almost never wrote references for others or requested them for myself – an approach I came to sorely regret when I founded Rethink and found myself wondering things like, 'Who was that woman from that European pharmaceutical company all those years ago? We worked really well together. What was her last name again?'"

Don't make her mistake! While originally LinkedIn was viewed simply as an employment vehicle, it has now been transformed into a substantive professional networking site. As you build your career, take the time to send a LinkedIn connection request to the people you work with or meet professionally. As we mention elsewhere in the book, one great place to find new clients (or employees!) is in businesses that you've worked with before.

These people already know and trust you and like your work – so make sure you have a way to get in contact with those people!

Once you're on LinkedIn, there are also active industry groups that may be relevant to your market and area of interest. These can be great ways to network and get to know other people in the field, not to mention keep up on new trends and developments.

A Caution: Social Media

Since we are all in the compliance profession, this probably goes without saying, but be cautious in mixing professional contacts and your personal social media.

Even if you like someone very much and have built a friendly working re-lationship, ask yourself: Do you want to know their politics or religion? Do you want them to know yours? Do you want them to see your vacations, the inside of your home, your friends and family members? Pictures of you out at happy hour or dancing at weddings?

Often, it's wise to keep the two separate. It's quite possible to have a ro-bust professional social media presence without ever mixing it with your personal social media activity.

Building an Online Brand

Once you've established your online presence as a business, you'll want to set your strategy for building and promoting your online brand – and po-tentially yourself, too, if that's part of your strategy.

Why does this matter? Done right, a great online presence can do some of the heavy lifting of attracting customers. A great online presence can get your company more exposure. It can give you authority and credibility in ways that matter. It can make the difference between a sales strategy where you cold-call uninterested prospects and one where interested pro-spects call you.

While we use the word "promoting," the best work in this area feels natural, human, and not "promote-y" at all. It's not about cornering people on the internet and forcing them to listen to you, like a talkative stranger at a party. In fact, you want to avoid that – when people use their online platforms just to broadcast product and sales information, they tend not to get much traction.

Instead, you want to find your way into the conversations your industry and market are already having and then figure out how to contribute something valuable to the dialogue.

Here are some tried and true tactics that can work:

Start a Blog with Great Content

As we cover in the chapter on writing, creating great content can demonstrate your experience and authority in your field. Informative or genuinely helpful blog posts can get passed around or found via a Google search – in fact, Kirsten met Kristy after finding one of her blog posts and making contact online.

Post Regularly to LinkedIn

LinkedIn posts and articles are a great way to start conversations and raise your visibility. Anyone who is connected to you will see these in their news feed. While posts have a word limit, articles can be any length – and they're a great way to showcase your thought leadership and industry knowledge. Plus, unlike print media, you can get immediate feedback and intelligent commentary. If you've written a blog post, be sure to post it to your LinkedIn feed for greater exposure.

Comment on or Share Other Posts

Regular LinkedIn activity can help raise your profile and also help you get to better know the people in your contact list. Once you're connected to someone, you'll see any articles, posts, and comments they contribute. Be generous – share articles and updates with your own contacts, take time to comment on posts, and engage in online conversations. It's possible to get to know people better and build your professional network just through these regular, small interactions. The same is true if your target market is on Twitter or another platform – get on there and join in the conversation. One method for increasing the reach of your LinkedIn posts is to share them on Twitter – an easy option on LinkedIn.

Write Guest Blogs or Appear on Podcasts

Others in your industry already have established platforms, like a well-known blog or a podcast. ("The FCPA Report" and the "Great Women in Compliance" podcasts are two examples, but there are many more.) And do you know what any regular content producer needs? More great content! Help them out by pitching a great blog post or lively conversation that's targeted to their audience. In return, you'll get in front of that audience, with the added credibility of being a featured writer or speaker.

What About Video and YouTube?

Should you consider using video on LinkedIn and/or having a YouTube presence? "One point to consider is that viewers are used to high-quality productions, so be sure to take some time either to learn how to do this or to retain someone who can produce videos professionally," Joe said.

When done well, videos certainly have the power to draw viewers and allow you to make a more personal impression. The conventional wisdom is to keep them short but, as with all other media, to provide valuable content.

Kristy produces a tremendous amount of video content. She's got hundreds of videos on her YouTube site. "During conferences, someone inevitably tells me they watch my videos every week. It's been great for me," said Kristy. Joe is correct though – they need to be professionally produced. "We built a filming studio in our house, and we have a computer dedicated entirely to editing and sound programs. It's been a big investment," said Kristy.

If You Start a Blog...

Having a good blog can be a massive boost to your business. To make the most of your blog, be sure to set it up to collect names and email addresses – typically called a mailing list. Services like Mailchimp and Constant Contact can make this easy. They will collect contact information from people who fill out the form to join your mailing list.

How do you get people to want to join your mailing list? First, you need to provide good content and value. But after that, you should add a pop-up asking people to join your list after they've been reading your site for a minute or more. Although people say they hate pop-ups, they work. Adding a pop-up will grow your audience infinitely more quickly than having a sign-up form on the side or bottom of your blog.

Your mailing list is like gold. If you've been providing value through blogs, then when you have a product to sell, you can launch it to an audience that is used to hearing from you and likes you. Study after study proves that email marketing sells more products than any other type of marketing, including social media sites like Instagram and Facebook.

If you do start a blog, post regularly and consistently – pick a cadence you can keep up and then stick with it. Readers will forget about you quickly if you don't post content regularly. "I send out an email every Wednesday with a one-minute video ("Wildly Effective Compliance Officer Tip of the Week") and a blog post. Sometimes I'm up at 2 a.m. finishing the blog post, but it is worth it. My audience expects to hear from me Wednesdays at noon Eastern. Consistency has helped me to build that following, and I don't want to jeopardize it!" said Kristy.

Consider whether you want your blog to be a personal blog or a blog on your business site. Kristy has both. Spark Compliance has its own blog, which tends to be content that has been posted on the Compliance Kristy site that has been altered to speak directly to a corporate audience instead of compliance officers. Her personal blog attracts much more traffic, but the Spark blog gives credibility to the company when potential clients are looking at the company site.

Becoming Recognizable, Likeable, and Credible

Like so many other things about starting a business, the most important part of establishing your online presence is simply getting started – getting online and getting active and then refining things from there.

Once you have a foundation in place, you can refine your online brand by focusing on the following three areas:

Be Even More Recognizable.

What makes your company distinctive?

From the start, Rethink Compliance stood out for its color scheme (turquoise and gray), its modern visuals, and its majority female workforce.

On the one hand, these elements should have nothing to do with creating great compliance content. On the other hand, the company was started as a direct response to market demand for a fresher, more modern approach. Seen in that light, each of these brand elements conveyed something important – that here was a fresh, modern, digitally-savvy option, not just the same old, same old.

As you look to refine your online brand and presentation, ask yourself: What's unique about your company? What are your most common visual elements – and do they stand out? How can you make it easy for people to recognize your brand?

And it's not just the visual details: Stories are a kind of brand. What stories do you tell about what you do and why you do it? Are there consistent elements you can play up or build on?

If you're recognizable, you're memorable (the opposite of forgettable!). You stand out in your field. You come to mind. These are all good things for gaining mindshare with your audience.

Make Your Brand Likable

The best online communicators are personable, casual, and human.

That human part is important! The best way to make your brand likable is to find ways to connect with your audience on a personal level.

People hate calling 1-800 customer service numbers at Giant Bank or Phone Company. They like doing business with other humans – especially humans they like.

A few ways to increase your likability:

Promote Yourself, Too

Earlier in the chapter, we talked about promoting both your company and yourself online. Promoting yourself can feel strange and awkward, even self-aggrandizing, especially if you've had largely behind-the-scenes roles in the past.

But giving your company a human face can really pay off. Picture two different consulting companies. Both have blogs and put out good content. But one company's leader is prominently featured on the website, often appears in short videos, often speaks at industry webinars, and is a frequent poster and commenter on LinkedIn. The other doesn't do any of this. Which company would you feel more comfortable calling up to discuss a consulting project? Probably one led by a person whose face and voice you've seen, especially if they seem to know what they're talking about.

Be Funny. Or Blunt. Or Opinionated.

In short, be real. The world is full of bland, manufactured content. Honesty and authenticity stand out and it builds trust when people feel like they are getting the full story.

Tell Stories

People remember and relate best to stories. You can tell stories about yourself and your experience in this field. Show some humility and how you learned from making mistakes at your own expense.

As David Hieatt, entrepreneur and founder of the DO Lectures in London says: "Being human is a superpower for brands. Because on the other side of every communication you send out is a human being."

Build Your Brand's Trust and Credibility

People buy from people they trust. People trusting your brand and finding it credible can have a profound effect on your bottom line.

To trust and believe in you, people want to know two things: First, that you know what you're doing. Second, that you genuinely care about their goals – and that their success is more important to you than simply closing a deal.

There are as many ways to express these two elements as there are businesses, so you'll want to tailor your approach to your specific competencies and company mission.

To communicate competence, try playing up your long-standing experience, emphasizing your credentials, or sharing case studies.

To communicate care, try writing blog posts that advocate for something your audience wants or even criticizing the ways it has been done poorly in the past.

As with likability, being human helps here also – people tend to trust others who they perceive as being authentic. Don't be afraid to show who you are. By being open about yourself, others will relate to you, which makes them much more likely to buy.

Humans move back and forth online, interacting with your brand and each other. Next, we'll explore one of the most important human business builders – networking.

Interview with Richard Bistrong, CEO, Front-Line Anti-Bribery LLC

Richard, you have more than 20,000 followers on LinkedIn, and at the time of publication you are rounding 10,000 Twitter followers! For those building a business, or getting ready to take the next step, why do you consider social media so important?

Thank you for the question! Social media is such an incredible platform for building your brand, making organic connections, and becoming a part of an incredibly robust ethics and compliance community, by sharing your perspective and work, but even more importantly, sharing that of others.

Is sharing the work of others just as important as sharing your own?

I think it's more important! And I'm not just speaking of likes or re-tweets – this is about deep engagement and interactions. For example, if you read an article that's interesting, or see it on LinkedIn or Twitter, instead of just liking or re-tweeting it, start a new thread. Share how the article impacted you, and how it might be helpful to your peers and colleagues.

Are there any 'best' practices in doing so?

Sure! For example, on LinkedIn, you have some word count to write something thoughtful, and by using the "@" you can hot-link in the author, or perhaps someone who has written on a similar topic, or even peers who you think might find it interesting. On Twitter you can also "@" the author, with a snippier summary, and on both LinkedIn and Twitter you can add hashtags that are followed. Yes, it takes more time than just hitting the "like" or "retweet" button, but by investing the time, you are creating a community, and by hot-linking the author(s). Even if you are not a direct connection, and when doing so you are creating what I often call a "social media handshake."

If I look back on being quoted in the Financial Times and The New York Times, among other periodicals and news channels, all of those connections started with organic social media interactions, where I was sharing the work of the journalists which ultimately led to them reaching out to me.

For LinkedIn, use images when you can. For example, if I'm attending an E&C conference, virtually or in person, and I am really moved by a presentation, I'll take a picture of the panel (easy to do with our smart phones). I'll post the image of the panel, and "@" the presenters, while sharing a summary of the take-aways. One of my favorites was from the SCCE when Kristy gave a keynote!

When traveling, attending a conference or an in-house event, even as a practitioner, don't be hesitant about taking a picture of you and some of your peers, attendees, etc., especially if there's an iconic background (a few of mine were the Great Wall of China and the Berlin Wall), and share some of what you learned while you were in that locale (of course get everyone's permission in advance, especially if it's in-house). Pictures of ourselves, our peers, and events humanize our work in the field, and show the 'person behind the brand!' One of my favorites was a dinner hosted by Kristy and I in Berlin at the SCCE ECEI [European Compliance & Ethics Institute], where Kirsten also joined us, and we snapped such a cool selfie after dinner, and had such a fun conversation about it on LinkedIn and Twitter!

Also, I can't echo your recommendations about LinkedIn group interactions enough (as opposed to just posting on your newsfeed). There are some great conversations on the groups, and remember, anyone who is in the group sees your post, even if you are not a first-degree connection, and it's a great way to build connections. Some are more active than others, so join a few dozen, and see what happens!

Any 'worst' practices?

Yes! Don't 'stuff' your posts with "@" hot-links to people and hashtags just to get 'likes' and 'attention.' Think of it as a conversation: If it's someone that you would want to know about the subject matter as if you were having a coffee, sure, add them in; but adding lines and lines of people and hashtags just to 'game' the algorithm, well, that's not organic or thoughtful.

The other is if someone is nice enough to comment on your post or tweet, as opposed to a 'like' or 're-tweet,' keep the conversation going! Even if it's just a thanks, take the time to acknowledge their engagement, and perhaps exchange perspectives on what they shared. I know, it takes time, but over time, being proactive, thoughtful and transparent, well, before you know it, you have a robust, vibrant, and engaged community of peers, colleagues, and perhaps future clients!

How about Instagram?

I would not discount it. In our field, for example, the E&C community in Brazil, specifically, and LATAM, more generally, is very engaged on Instagram. And while it's more of a challenge to put in links to articles, etc., it's a fun way via images to share your work and practice.

And video?

It's powerful, but no video is better than bad video. There are media best practices, including lighting, sound, and background, among others, that need to be carefully considered before posting video. If you want to see a great example, check out Kristy's YouTube channel!

What about the link between meeting people (in person or virtually) and social media?

Once again, it needs to be nuanced, thoughtful and organic. I have a workflow: When I collect business cards, for example at events, when I return home, I will send them an invitation to connect on LinkedIn, with a personalized invitation (not the LinkedIn template), with a thank you for taking the time to chat, inviting them to connect, and will do the same on other social media platforms, e.g., Instagram, Twitter, etc.

CHAPTER 13

Networking

Author Porter Gale was right – your network is your net worth. There is little as important to an entrepreneur as a healthy network. Networking frequently has a bad reputation. Like sales, it can be seen as sleazy and self-serving. But it doesn't have to be! Networking done well benefits everyone involved.

There are many benefits to networking. Networking can help when looking for potential partners, employees, contractors, references, and/or customers. It can help you keep up to speed on the market, including learning about new developments, trends, and approaches.

Aside from any specific business objective, there is comfort in being able to compare notes and experiences with others in our profession. This is especially helpful if you have set up your own shop and don't want to feel isolated.

There are many specific ways to use networking. Here are just a few:

A Bridge to Other Authors

A great way to network is to get in touch with authors in the industry. If you're researching a particular topic because you're interested in it or you want to write about it yourself, you'll likely be reading others' work. You may find you have questions or new ideas related to the topic. This can provide a good bridge for communicating with the author.

Let's say you read a useful article in SCCE's *Compliance and Ethics Professional Magazine* about the state of whistleblower law in the US, and you've also been reading about the EU's whistleblower directive. This could be a perfect opportunity for communicating with the author to discuss how EU law compares with American law.

Where might this take you? The author may know of companies instituting whistleblower systems and might be a referral source for you. She might direct you to new sources that could enhance your own research and knowledge. You might at some point even become co-authors. The one thing you know for sure is that if the author does not know that you exist, there is nothing she can or will do for you or your business.

Do not be reluctant to contact authors or those who are mentioned in articles. But remember once again to focus on adding value. Make sure you know something about the topic first. Before you reach out, consider what you have to contribute. You may have read a different article on the same subject, and you could contact the author about that other piece. Give some serious thought and time to this, as you do not want to pursue trivial points. But if you are genuinely adding value in some way, even a cold outreach is likely to be appreciated by the author.

A Bridge to Other Speakers

You can use a similar process regarding expert speakers in your field.

When you're at a conference or watching a webinar, listen carefully to the speaker and take detailed notes of interesting points. You can then contact the speaker, noting what you learned from the presentation. As with written materials, you can start a dialogue about areas of common interest, especially if you have new ideas or information to offer.

As we covered in detail in the section about online presence, many people in the compliance profession are active on LinkedIn. This site provides a way to get in contact with those speakers. Once linked, you can extend your connection by liking or commenting on their posts.

An Unexpected Bridge to New Clients

When networking, remember to play the long game. Remember that this is a small industry, and you may encounter the same people many times as all of your careers develop.

If you want to prospect for clients or customers, there will be some people in your network who will be obvious potential prospects. But you do not want to make assumptions about people's value. Someone who is not a decision maker today may become one down the road.

Joe remembers one sales call with a potential customer for Integrity Interactive at a company in the Chicago area. He and an Integrity colleague presented on all that their company had to offer. The two company representatives – lawyers – were polite and interested but did not choose to use Integrity's services.

A few years passed, and one of those two lawyers took up a compliance job at another company. Joe and his colleague must have made a good impression because he contacted Joe to do work for that new client. The same person later moved to an even bigger company, and the same thing happened.

The same could be true of a law student who shows interest in the field of compliance and ethics. If you provide advice and assistance, the person may appreciate it, but never follow up with you. But there will also be some who remember and make a point of appreciating those who have helped them. That person may later be successful in a career in compliance and ethics and remember your help.

Know that each person in your network may be important at some time in the future, in ways you cannot foresee now.

You Need a System

To enhance your networking, there is great value in having an organized system for keeping track of those in your network. Your network list and system can be an extremely valuable asset of your business. You do not want to spare attention to this. Your record may keep track of business in-teractions and also personal information. You should, for example, note each person's professional interests, and personal information you hear from them such as where they live or the name of their spouse. It's much more personal to ask how Brandon is than to open with "what have you been up to?"

Kristy instituted a professional online system to track her leads. "I got frustrated that I'd met so many people over the years at conferences, and I didn't have a systematic way to get ahold of them. I have my assistant add new contacts into the system so that we can stay in touch. The system even alerts me to follow up after I've made someone's acquaintance. It's been a game-changer."

You can use anything, from a paper Rolodex to an Excel sheet to a fancy online program like Salesforce. Whatever you do, begin now. Even if you think you'll remember everyone you meet, put their contacts in one place so you can find them when you need them.

There's No One Way to Network

You don't need to be a "people person" to network! In fact, there are as many different styles of networking as there are personality types.

Those who are more extroverted may be drawn to social events and fun activities. For those more introverted, there are means to touch base regu-larly with more focus on professional matters.

When you have your own business, people are likely to be at least a bit suspicious and may assume you just want to sell them something. This calls for thoughtful timing, so you are not contacting someone for the first time in years just to ask them to buy something. It is important to have a trusting relationship first.

Giving to Get

If you have followed the advice earlier in this book, you have developed expertise and ways you can be of value to others in the field. During your networking, it is important that you find a way to benefit the other person, not just yourself. Especially if you are a vendor, figure out how to contribute something beyond just a sales pitch.

If you learn of a new development related to compliance, for example a new training resource, pass it along to your network. But don't use it as an obvious pitch to get them to come to you. Instead, add value by giving them ideas on what to do in response to the new development.

When you engage in networking, remember that while you want to add value, this is not an invitation to show off or simply try to impress others with your expertise. One of the most important skills in networking is listening. It may seem counterintuitive, but if you want to impress people with your knowledge and expertise, one of the best ways to do this is to listen intelligently. Show that you are smart enough to understand what the other person is saying.

A classic way to demonstrate your understanding of the other person is to restate back to that person what they are saying. This cannot be a mindless, rote exercise. It takes actual thinking about what the person has said or written. But if done well, it has two benefits. First, you understand better what the person is saying and are more likely to have learned something by doing this. And, second, you validate the other person. If you know your field, you will typically be able to add something or offer an example that fits – or even expands – the other person's thinking.

Other Great Networking Opportunities

There are countless networking opportunities.

Live Events

Even in the internet era, there remains tremendous value in live events. These include conferences such as those operated by SCCE. Whether they are enormous gatherings run by institutes that draw thousands of participants from around the world, or local gatherings at a luncheon, they can be worth your time and attention.

To maximize the benefit of live events, it is good to prepare and have a game plan. Determine in advance what you would like to achieve at the event, and identify specific individuals you would like to meet. Pursue this when you can, but also be open to other possibilities that may develop during the gathering.

If you want to meet someone speaking at or attending an event, send them an email or LinkedIn message beforehand saying you hope that you'll see them or making a plan to meet up at a coffee break. Take advantage of any built-in networking opportunities, like the speed networking event the SCCE offers.

The reason this strategy is so effective is that it will hone your energy so that you don't end up mindlessly staring at the coffee station not meeting anyone. By creating a networking strategy, you'll make the most of your time at events.

Networking Online

There are also numerous opportunities to network online, including commenting on others' blogs. In addition to posting your own informative pieces, you can target specific exchanges with other commentators whose backgrounds are interesting to you.

LinkedIn is currently the leading general forum for this. You can focus on specific groups on LinkedIn that match your areas of interest. These may be organized by geographic area, subject/risk area (e.g., antitrust, money laundering, privacy, etc.), or compliance function (e.g., compliance officers, investigators).

Here it is essential to remember the point about adding value. When you learn of new developments, when you see useful tools for practitioners, when you find a new resource, consider sharing these with your LinkedIn connections. Avoid telling people that you are an expert; instead, show them by sharing useful information on LinkedIn.

While In-House

Prioritize building your network while you are in-house. Many of your first customers will come from your network.

"The first few months of Spark Compliance were terrifying. I wouldn't have gotten through without my network referring work to me and offering to act as references who could validate my credibility as a practitioner. Without them, I don't think we would have made it six months," said Kristy.

Similarly, at Rethink, many of Kirsten's earliest customers were either former colleagues, former clients, or referrals from those friends or clients. Even today, these represent a large proportion of the business.

Finally, if you are still in-house, consider networking opportunities with the vendors who service your company. While you want to avoid any conflicts of interest and should put the interests of your employer first, you should not dismiss vendors as only being salespeople. The principles discussed above also apply to those who are currently suppliers and potential suppliers to your current employer. Treat them with respect, listen to them, and have them in your network database. They may, in turn, find their next job in a company that could be a potential customer for your new business.

CHAPTER 14

Organizations and Groups

Helen Keller said that "alone we can do so little, together we can do so much." Working with organizations and groups in the industry can expand your horizons exponentially. Groups can increase your networking opportunities, give you information on the latest happenings in the industry, and provide you with a ready place for resources.

The Impetus to Create Compliance-Related Groups

The defense industry scandals in the 1980s threatened the legitimacy of the entire industry. The major defense contractors came together to form a group called the Defense Industry Initiative (DII). All of the signatories agreed to follow a set standard in their approaches to compliance. Among these was a commitment to participate in an annual best practices forum where they would talk about and share their efforts to achieve best practices in their compliance programs. The idea was to have a free and open exchange.

In the beginning of the 1990s, when the US Sentencing Commission was developing its standards for criminal penalties for organizations, part of its analysis was informed by the experience of the defense industry in the DII. The thinking was that companies' compliance efforts should be at least as good as the general industry approach. Of course, to know what other companies were doing required everyone to be willing to share their own experiences. This led to a provision now contained in the Sentencing Guidelines notes that states:

> Commentary note 2:
> (B) Applicable Governmental Regulation and Industry Practice. – An organization's failure to incorporate and follow applicable industry practice or the standards called for by any applicable governmental regulation weighs against a finding of an effective compliance and ethics program. [10]

In other words, companies need to know what is going on in the industry and be at least that good. This provided a push for companies to be open about what they were doing in their programs. To this day it remains a strength. Anyone who has attended a compliance conference would agree, this openness is constantly on display.

International Expansion of Openness Among Colleagues

These experiences were also followed in the international field. In the good practice guidance issued by the Organisation for Economic Co-operation and Development (OECD)'s working group on bribery, which serves as a guide for anti-corruption compliance programs, item 12 calls for:

> 12. periodic reviews of the ethics and compliance programmes or measures, designed to evaluate and improve their effectiveness in preventing and detecting foreign bribery, taking into account relevant developments in the field, and evolving international and industry standards. [11]

Soon the world's compliance officers began working in groups to learn from each other. Organizations formalized around them, and industry groups were born.

Looking for Groups

One of the first things to understand when looking for potential groups is that the groups' names may vary significantly, and there may be differences in emphasis.

While the words "compliance and ethics" are common, there may be variations using such words as "integrity," "business ethics," "governance" and "risk." "GRC" is common, as in Australia's GRC Institute, with the acronym standing for "governance, risk, and compliance." There are also groups based on compliance function, geography, and risk area.

The Importance of Working with Established Groups

Working with established groups can rocket your success. Why is it so important to know about and work with these groups? There are several reasons. They represent an important opportunity to meet and recruit potential clients. You can find out about pending business opportunities, such as a company's interest in having someone conduct an outside assessment. There are also potential business partners, including those who may provide you valuable resources or who may work with you on teams. These groups can also provide you valuable market input about what others are doing in the marketplace and which market needs are not yet being met.

For Kirsten, speaking to compliance organizations landed Rethink some of its earliest non-network leads. In 2017, she flew to Ohio to speak to the Ohio Regional Corporate Counsel Association (ORCCA) and wound up doing business with two of the companies at the event, then another four that she met through those companies on return trips to Cleveland.

Similarly, Rethink did its first SCCE webinar in August of 2016 and it brought in six clients over the next 18 months. After that, Rethink made it a priority to speak and write for SCCE. Rethink also paid to have a booth at the national conference from 2016, and each year that brought in a number of the next year's clients.

"If you're looking to expand beyond your network, speaking, writing and advertising with compliance groups and industry associations will get you in front of a wide audience of people you've never met," Kirsten said.

Expanding Professional Opportunities with Established Groups

Professional groups can provide opportunities beyond making personal contacts. Many offer opportunities to write and speak, including live presentations, podcasts, and online presentations. There are even times when a group may play a role in creating or expanding a market.

One of the distinctive elements of the compliance and ethics profession is the willingness to share experiences with their peers. Perhaps it reflects the nature of the field. Compliance professionals can find themselves feeling outside the normal business flow in their own companies or organizations. They may be the ones challenging accepted ways of doing things or raising questions about ambitious business plans. At those times we may need to look outside the corporate walls for validation.

When Joe was in the early telecommunications compliance practices forum, he would often have the "is it them or is it me?" discussions with concerned peers. Colleagues at other companies can give the reassurance necessary to persevere in times of challenge and stress.

Finding the Right Group

There are many different groups and places to look for groups.

Compliance Industry Associations

Organizations that are focused on compliance are an obvious place to start. At the time of this writing, these include:

- Society of Corporate Compliance & Ethics (SCCE), mentioned several times in this book (Joe and Kristy have both served on the board)

- Health Care Compliance Association (HCCA), the SCCE's sister organization
- Ethics & Compliance Initiative (ECI)
- Compliance Week
- Ethisphere

These organizations offer a broad range of outlets and opportunities for compliance and ethics professionals.

For those interested in writing and connecting with experts in the field, there are publications like *Compliance and Ethics Professional Magazine* (CEP), *Ethikos*, and *Compliance Week*. Joe is the editor in chief of *Compliance and Ethics Professional Magazine* and was an editor of *Ethikos* in its prior incarnation.

These organizations also publish books and white papers, maintain blogs and websites, record podcasts, and have a presence on social media sites like LinkedIn, Twitter, and others. Creating material for any of these channels provides a good outlet for reaching compliance and ethics professionals globally.

Finally, compliance industry organizations offer a range of conferences throughout the US and around the world. These range from small, city-based gatherings of a few dozen people to thousands of attendees at some of the bigger national conferences.

Joining the Board

Several organizations offer leadership opportunities by joining the board of directors.

Being on the board can be a major advantage for networking. First, there is prestige from showing leadership in the profession. But there is also excellent networking potential on the board itself. You can hear from leaders in the field about trends that affect the profession, and there may also be opportunities to make important partner and client connections.

It is important to note that it may take more than one application to get on to the board. Kristy was only selected after her second application. "It was discouraging not to be chosen immediately, but I doubled-down on the work I was doing in the profession to be even more qualified the next year."

Legal Networking Groups

For lawyers, there are good opportunities in professional groups. In the US, the American Bar Association (ABA), through its various sections, can provide a good networking vehicle. For example, the ABA's Antitrust Section has its own compliance and ethics committee. This group has put on presentations about compliance at section national meetings and has published books and white papers. It has also published its own newsletter, which offers opportunities for compliance lawyers to get exposure to the field. The Business Law Section has published articles related to compliance in its magazine. For instance, Joe recently co-authored a piece that was published as we were writing this book.

For in-house counsel, the Association of Corporate Counsel (ACC) – https://www.acc.com) –and its publications offer a useful vehicle. When Joe was in-house, he publicized his first book through writing for the *ACC Docket*. He was also able to present on the topic of his book at ACC conferences. In fact, an article Joe wrote was included by the ACC in its influential filing with the Sentencing Commission when the commission was first considering the role of compliance programs. Much of Joe's network developed through the ACC.

Separate from the ABA and ACC are the individual state bar groups. These also put on seminars and have publications. Joe, as a member of the Pennsylvania bar, had an early article about the book, *Interactive Corporate Compliance*, used as the cover story for the Pennsylvania Bar Association's magazine.

Control-Oriented Professional Groups

Just as is the case for lawyers, other control-oriented professional groups also have organizations and can provide similar opportunities. The opportunities for networking in these groups are considerable. These include the Association of Certified Fraud Examiners (https://www.acfe.com), the Society of Human Resources Management (https://www.shrm.org), and organizations of internal investigators.

Local Compliance and Ethics Groups

In addition to the global and national groups, there are also local ones. These can be especially important if you want a local focus in your marketing. Don't forget that the local group may include members that work for national and global companies.

Early on, Joe worked with the Delaware Valley chapter of the ACC to form one of the first local compliance and ethics group. This committee staged an early symposium on the subject, working with the University of Pennsylvania Law School. Again, as was true for ACC, contacts here proved valuable for Joe once he was out in private practice.

Today there are such local groups in other key locations. For example, there is Greater Houston Business Ethics Roundtable (GHBER) in Houston, the Atlanta Compliance and Ethics (ACE) Roundtable in Atlanta, and a similar group in Chicago. In fact, in the course of conducting a review of a US company's compliance operations in Europe, a colleague of Joe's discovered that the company's Paris office had helped form a Paris-area compliance group.

Wherever you live, do not assume such a group does not exist until you check. And if there is no such group, you might consider creating one!

Industry-Specific Groups

From what may be considered the beginning of the modern era in compliance and ethics, there have been industry-specific compliance and ethics groups. Just like the Defense Industry Initiative described earlier in this chapter, compliance professionals in a single industry often create forums for conversation, best-practice sharing, and networking. If such a group does not yet exist in your industry, consider creating one.

Industry groups can offer great opportunities. For instance, at the time of the onset of the sentencing guidelines, Joe and another lawyer in the telecommunications industry decided to follow the defense industry model and formed the Telecommunications Compliance Practices Forum. This was a relatively small group of compliance practitioners in what were then the "landline" companies in that industry. They met a few times a year and exchanged information, ideas and experiences. These contacts were also important for Joe in private practice.

Later on, Joe was recruited to be the antitrust lawyer for the Pharmaceutical Industry Compliance Practices Forum. As was true for the other groups, this was also an important source of client work.

Specialist Groups

Finally, there are groups based on the various compliance risk areas. One of the largest is the International Association of Privacy Professionals (IAPP) (https://iapp.org). IAPP offers a certification related to compliance in the privacy area. IAPP conferences can be a key source of contacts for those interested in this specific field. Money laundering is another area with a broad-based organization, as is securities law. Workplace safety and environmental compliance also have their own groups.

Once in any of these groups, there is value in playing a leadership role. This can develop from offering to help in the organization and by promoting its agenda. Leadership can be developed through writing for the group's publication or blog, and speaking, especially in conferences, webinars, and podcasts. Such leadership can provide excellent visibility and enhanced opportunities for networking. Just as is true for winning over clients, the best way to become connected with any organization is to offer value.

SECTION FOUR:
Exit

When you're just starting out, the idea of quitting your business or selling it may be the last thing on your mind. But, as you'll see in the last section of this book, beginning with the end in mind may be one of the best things you can do to ensure long-term success.

CHAPTER 15

Selling the Business

It is often said that the most important part of starting a business is having what's known as an "exit strategy." An exit strategy is a plan for how the business will end, either by selling it, dissolving it, letting it simply die down, giving it to employees, or allowing them to buy it.

Exit strategies are important, so as you're starting your business, consider how you might end it.

If you don't plan for a future sale of the business, you may end up at some time walking away and losing what would have been a valuable asset had you planned differently. In time you may decide to retire or otherwise move on. The value of the business may evaporate when you leave unless you have planned this well.

In 2017, Kirsten did an accounting check-up that was really a business review from a finance perspective. The accountant was someone who had grown and sold multiple businesses. The first thing he asked was, "What is your five-year plan?" And when she opened her mouth to answer, he continued and said, "If you're about to say anything other than selling the business, it's the wrong answer. If you create a business you can sell, the fundamentals will be right and you can sell or keep running it profitably forever – you have options. But if you create a business you can't sell, you have no options and it's probably not a very good business."

Starting with the assumption you may someday sell the business is a useful frame of mind. It does not mean you ultimately have to sell, but it does mean that if you want to, you will be able to.

Be sure to discuss this strategy of planning to sell the business early on with your lawyer and your accountant. Find someone with the expertise to guide you on how to take the business in this direction from the beginning.

Selling a Product-Based Business vs. a Consulting Firm

There are many differences between selling a product-based company versus selling a consulting or other professional services firm.

Selling a Product-Based Firm

Selling a product-based firm is often easier than selling a professional services/consulting firm.

This is because the revenue comes directly from the product, not the relationship with the individual consultant or group. If your product involves recurring revenue, meaning that the contracts with customers provide for a multi-month or year commitment, then your business will typically be worth more than products that are sold on a one-time basis.

Joe's Story

"At Integrity Interactive, we planned to sell right from the beginning, so we designed the business that way. This was during the dot-com era when investors were pouring cash into anything that looked like an internet business no matter how much money it was losing, so we joked about first losing a ton of money, then doing an IPO and retiring rich. However, we were cash positive from early on and the business actually made money. Unlike much of the dot-com hype, we were a real business.

"When Kirk and I decided to ask Carl Nelson to join us as CEO, it was with that clear intention of selling the business. We knew that Carl had done this type of thing before, would understand our plan, and would know how to execute it. We welcomed the fact that he could do this better than we could. Plus, he had experience in producing training materials. He knew how to obtain resources at bargain-basement prices, and he knew when and how to hire excellent talent.

"We made sure that we had a professional CFO to be certain our numbers were transparent and always made sense. We also had good legal counsel (even though Kirk and I are both lawyers). We followed the formalities in the operation of the business, so we had regular board meetings and kept minutes."

The key thing about structuring a product-based business to sell is that it helps you make the business self-sufficient and not reliant on you. It allows you to think clearly. For instance, if you can hire someone more talented than you, that is ok because it adds to the value of the business.

Joe reminisced, "What Integrity Interactive offered was like a product, but with a continuing revenue stream. While we did a good job managing and growing it, none of us who started it were indispensable. The business would generate cash from its existing base without us. That was by design – it was salable and scalable. A potential purchaser could see that all it needed to continue as a money-making business was sufficient management skill."

Selling a Consulting Business

Selling a consulting business, or a business that strongly relies on you, can be challenging. After all, if you leave, then what is the draw for existing and future customers? Even though it can be difficult, it is possible to sell a consulting/professional services firm. There are several ways to do this.

One of the most common ways to sell a consulting business is to be purchased by one of your competitors. This can happen when a larger consulting firm wants to expand its client base, geographical footprint, or areas of specialty. They may simply want to stop having to compete with you!

Other times consulting businesses are sold to companies in a different part of the compliance ecosystem. "We were approached by a large financial services consulting firm to see if we were open to purchasing," said Kristy. "They were interested in us because we represented immediate access to the corporate compliance world, complete with a large client roster. They wanted to look for cross-selling opportunities and to benefit from the Spark

Compliance reputation. It was worth it for them to pay a premium so they did not have to build the base themselves."

One of the negative things about starting a consulting business is the low multiplier for which it sells. You will likely only get between three-quarters and twice annual revenue as the sale price. This is dramatically outstripped by product-focused businesses like training courses or software, which may sell for many times its annual revenue.

Should I Stay or Should I Go Now?

One big question in contemplating the sale of a business is whether you will stay on after the sale or not. There are strong pros and cons for both approaches.

If You Stay

You staying on may be a condition of the sale. This can be very flattering – the purchasers value your expertise. More often than not, if you sell your consulting business, expect that you'll be roped into a 12-, 24-, or 36-month contract with the new firm.

Unlike software or other products that can be immediately sold to the public or other businesses, professional service firms create long-term individualized trust between the client and the consultant. For the buyer to maximize the value of the business and client relationships, they will almost always tie the owner up in a contract that pays out some money up-front but keeps an additional amount until the end of the contractual period to ensure you stay and do your best work for the buyer.

Regardless of whether it is contractually mandated, you may want to stay on to guide the ship that you've created through its transition. But remember, you are no longer in charge. Somebody with enough money to buy your business may not necessarily be entrepreneurial or the type of person you want to work with. Even if they initially want you to stay on, you should be realistic. They may ultimately decide they know better than you or they just don't need you. They may love you at first, but don't count on that lasting.

If You Go

When it comes time to think about selling the business, there are certain negative aspects to bear in mind. It can be an emotional process; you may consider this business to be your legacy.

Many entrepreneurs are shocked at how lost they feel once they sell their business. The thing that they thought about constantly that occupied the majority of their time is gone. Sometimes entrepreneurs face a loss of identity. If they're not the owner of their business, who are they?

Then there is the issue of employees. There are people you hired and grew to really appreciate. They become your colleagues and friends. When you sell your business, you also sell control of their work conditions to someone else. Many times, the purchaser of the business will make immediate redundancies to save cash. For instance, if your venture is sold to a larger company that already has its own HR and finance personnel, your equivalent department may immediately face unemployment. That knowledge can be stressful and may play a part in your decision-making.

If you've made a deal to sell, just as they say for retirement, plan on what you are going to do next, both if you stay for a period of time and if you completely separate yourself from the business. On the latter, be sure you have a place to direct your energy. This is not as simple as it might seem at first. It is not easy to go from being a driven entrepreneur one day to a retired ex-businessperson the next. After you choose to sell, ultimately all you will have are memories and money.

Can You Start Again?

You will likely have to agree to a non-compete, which can be very constraining. And unlike many employment non-competes which may be unenforceable depending on state law, those associated with the sale of a business stand on firmer footing. After all, someone is putting up good money based on the value of the business, and if you compete with that, it undermines the value of what the purchaser got for their money.

You want to be very clear on the non-compete. Have a lawyer who knows this area and has experience with it review your draft contract. Also, work out ownership of intellectual property, so you are not permanently constrained from participating in the field. Be sure, for example, that you are free to write, speak, and teach if those things appeal to you. Don't assume that just because you sold the business that you will never be interested in being in this field again. If you do need to agree to a non-compete, remember that the scope and length of time are negotiable, but the scope and length can influence the price the buyers will pay. However, if the buyer does not feel threatened by the prospect of you returning to the marketplace, then they may not be as concerned about a lengthy and strong non-compete.

Is it Enough?

Kristy remembers hearing an entrepreneur on a podcast talking about his regret in selling his business. He'd built an online company and sold it for $800,000. He was elated until he realized that he couldn't live off that for many years, even if it were to be well invested (especially after tax was removed). He said he should have waited until he had "f-you money," which meant enough that if it were well invested, he could live off the interest for the rest of his life. He was frustrated that he had to start over and build a new venture, which could take many years, or get a job where he'd likely feel stifled.

When you sell your business, you'll be starting over in many ways. If you don't sell it for "enough," you may have to start over. Remember that most entrepreneurs can't take money out of their ventures for months or even years while they build them up. If the offer doesn't yield enough money to drop out, it may not be worth taking.

It Will Take More Time Than You Think

When you have reached the point where you believe you can sell the business, don't count on doing this quickly. It can take substantial diligence before the potential buyer is satisfied. Don't spend the proceeds of the sale until they are actually in your account. Much can happen, even right before a deal is supposed to close.

Joe noted, "With Integrity Interactive we had one contingency after another come up in the deal-making process. At some point, we were practically waiting for the buyer to require us to coverage of the contingency of a giant comet colliding with the earth! But fortunately, they missed that one. It seemed as if they covered every other possible scenario. Since we had experienced deal people working with us, no contingency was triggered and we received every dollar we had negotiated for."

Selling your business is a major milestone, both in the life of the business and in your own life. With thoughtful planning, you can set yourself up for an excellent exit.

Great Advice

A few additional points from an angel investor and former business partner in Integrity Interactive, Kirk Jordan:

The angel investment community has grown dramatically in recent years. Angel investors are individuals who provide capital early in a company's history, typically in exchange for convertible debt or equity. If you need funds to grow your business before getting to a final "exit" event, angel investors are something you should consider. Most major metropolitan areas have angel investment groups. Check out the Angel Capital Association (ACA) website https://www.angelcapitalassociation.org for more information.

If you do take investment capital in exchange for equity in your company (either from angel investors or others), it is important that your interests and goals are aligned with your investors. For example, your investors will invest for the primary reason of ultimately receiving a return on their investment, which will typically occur when the company is sold (or if there is an IPO, though this is relatively rare). Thus, if your ultimate goal is not to sell the company, you should carefully consider whether you want to take outside investment, as you may end up losing majority control of the company. In that case, the company could be subject to sale without your consent.

As you grow the company, experienced outside board members can be a great asset. If you take investment from an angel investment group, for example, the group may be able to provide a board member with experience and contacts in your industry/field. The board members can help introduce you to potential customers, strategic partners, and potential acquirers.

If you start your company to ultimately sell it, you should cultivate relationships with potential acquirers early in your company's history (of course, always be aware of potential antitrust issues). Strong relationships take time to develop, so start early. For example, it is not unusual for the buyer of a company to be a strategic partner with whom the purchased company previously had a distribution, reseller, or similar relationship.

At Integrity Interactive, we took an investment from two private equity groups, before ultimately selling to a strategic investor (in this case, a competitor in our industry). Private equity is typically composed of funds and investors that directly invest in private companies. Unlike angel investors, who invest their own funds, private equity investors usually invest "other people's money." This is the same for venture capital (VC) investors. As a general rule, VC funds look to invest more substantial amounts than private equity or angel investors.

If you get to the point where you think your company is a good candidate for either private equity or VC investment, consider hiring an advisory firm with experience in selling or "shopping" companies in your industry. A good advisory firm can be well worth the cost (typically a small percentage of the sale). The firm will help you prepare your "pitch" book and presentations and can solicit interest and offers from a wide array of potential buyers. One of the key advantages of this approach is that your advisor can generate an auction-like environment among potential acquirers, resulting in the highest potential price for the business.

CHAPTER 16

The Beginning and the End

C Congratulations! You've reached the end of the beginning, and now it's time for the real fun to start. Jumping into entrepreneurship will change your life completely. By reading this book, you have chosen to educate yourself, which is half the battle. You've made yourself much more likely to succeed, and you should be proud of that.

Preparing for the Rollercoaster

Being an entrepreneur often feels like being on a rollercoaster. Some moments you feel on top of the world and like you can conquer anything. Other moments you feel so low you could cry at the drop of a hat or hide beneath the bedsheets and never come out. The emotional journey of entrepreneurship is profound.

The High Highs

Becoming your own boss can give you a tremendous sense of freedom, particularly if you hated your job. Putting up your website, winning your first client, and earning your first money as an owner are huge milestones that often come with euphoria.

"I loved the meetings I had with my partners the first year. The whole world had so much possibility. I felt like a maverick, and it was thrilling," said Kristy.

"I still remember the first time a client used 'Rethink' in a meeting. She was telling her colleagues 'Rethink specializes in x, and Rethink will do y for us.' And I thought to myself: I made up that name on a plane last year, and now all these people see it as something real," Kirsten said.

The Low Lows

For most entrepreneurs, the high highs come with equally low lows. Entrepreneurs have twice the levels of depression as the general population. The act of starting a business can create enormous stress. One article noted that "long hours, poor sleep habits, and an often-lacking social life contribute to a significant decline in mental health for entrepreneurs. One Canadian study found that 62% of business owners felt depressed at least once a week."[12]

Two months after starting Spark Compliance, Kristy found herself panicking at three in the morning in a hotel room in the Czech Republic at a conference. She called her mother in California, who immediately asked if Kristy had been in an accident or arrested given the tenor of Kristy's voice. "I was not prepared for the fear of failure, nor for the lack of control created by suddenly not having a paycheck," said Kristy.

Knowing that it is normal to have high highs and low lows can make the transition to entrepreneurship more manageable. Over time you may even begin to enjoy the cycle, as downtimes tend to lead to growth and new opportunities.

Not Everyone Will Understand

Many people fantasize about starting a business, but relatively few actually do it (especially full-time). When you start, you may be confronted by well-meaning friends and family members fearing for you. They may send you statistics about the number of small business failures and tell you about their friend-of-a-friend who lost everything when his business failed and had to file bankruptcy.

"A few months after starting Spark, my sister called and told me she'd found me a job to apply to in New York. I told her I had created my company and was sticking with it. 'But you have to have a job!' she said. It took a long time for her to understand that I *had* a job – I made it for myself," said Kristy.

When others overlay their doubt on you, remember that it probably comes from a place of love. They want you to be safe, but safety is probably not what you're going for if you decide to start a business. Excitement, the opportunity for endless growth, the chance to continuously learn, and the ability to affect hundreds or even thousands of people are probably a much higher priority for you than safety.

Don't expect everyone to understand your choices or motivations. Keep your "why" upfront in your mind. Remember why it is so important for you to have a successful business. This will keep you going when the going gets tough.

Things to Remember

We've covered a lot of territory in this book. From conceiving your dream to executing your digital marketing plan, you're ready to go. But before you do, we each want to leave you with our top three tips.

Kirsten's Top Three Tips

- Focus first on finding product-market fit. If you nail this, you will buy yourself time and margin to figure out the rest.

- Don't feel like you need to know everything to start – you can learn (you will have to learn!) as you go.

- Expect to be stretched in both the best and most humbling ways possible. You'll be both better and worse at this than you imagined.

Kristy's Top Three Tips

- Always keep on top of your cash flow. If possible, keep a rolling 12-week forecast. If you know when you're going to face lean times, you can prepare for them.

- Content marketing is key in this industry. Strive to be a thought leader and to create great blogs, books, white papers, or other materials.

- Don't be afraid to have a distinctive point of view. Differentiating yourself from the crowd will draw business to you if it's done professionally.

Joe's Top Three Tips

- For introverts, be proud of what you are. Just team with someone who likes the other stuff that is not your strength.

- Network with the people in your field. Be curious and add value for others. When you read something interesting or hear something, write to the author or speaker.

- Pick an area and master it. Kill it. Know everyone in the area and know more about that area than anyone else could know.

There's a lot to learn about entrepreneurship, so please keep using this book as a guide. Re-read pertinent sections as new issues come up. The word "iterative" is frequently used in relation to start-ups. It simply means starting with one thing and continuing to update, refresh, and grow it in stages. Your business will be iterative, and the passages most useful to you in the beginning may not be the same as those most useful to you in three months or three years.

The Time is Now

As noted in the introduction, there is never a perfect time to start a business. If you let fear control you, running worst-case scenarios in your head over and over again, you'll never fulfill the longing in your heart to start living your dream. Robert Kiyosaki, the author of *Rich Dad, Poor Dad*, said, "Everyone can tell you the risk. Entrepreneurs can see the reward."

For Joe, Kirsten, and Kristy, the risk has turned out to be very rewarding. None of them would change their stories or go back to life with a nine-to-five job. "Creating and growing a business has been exhilarating, terrifying, fascinating, and never once boring, and it has taught me so much. Now that I've done it, I can't imagine doing anything else," Kirsten says. Joe agreed, noting, "When I started out, I wondered if there would be a morning when I woke up and missed going to a job, having a paycheck and a boss. That was 25 years ago, and so far there hasn't been one single day when I had that thought."

> *"Everyone can tell you the risk. Entrepreneurs can see the reward."*
> *- Robert Kiyosaki*

Begin where you are. Write your business plan, put together your website, write a great piece of content to get people talking. We're rooting for you! We know you can do it!

Acknowledgements

Kristy Grant-Hart

Writing this book has been the culmination of a lifelong pull toward entrepreneurship. I couldn't have reached this place without the extraordinary support of my husband Jonathan Grant-Hart.

Thank you to my family for your unwavering support, especially to my mother, Kathy Elwood, who continues to be the biggest cheerleader I could ever hope for. To my sisters, Kelly and Kimberly, and to their families, thank you for listening to all of my crazy ideas and for believing in dreams coming true. Also to the Harts, my loving in-laws, and to my father, who I know is rooting for me from the other side.

I am so grateful for my mentors in business, including Greg Gershuni, who gave me my first job in the law, working as his administrative assistant, and to Debra Wong Yang, who to this day inspires me with her legal mastery and enthusiasm for life. I am richer for having worked with you both. Thank you also to Lisa Beth Lentini, who gave me my first job in the compliance world and who responded with jubilance when I told her that I was going out on my own. I'll never forget that.

To my fantastic co-authors: Joe Murphy – your insight and brilliance is unparalleled. Thank you for your championing of me. Kirsten – we started this crazy thing nearly at the same time. I'm so lucky to call you my friend. I respect you both so enormously.

Thank you to the remarkable people in the compliance world that have helped me along, especially Richard Bistrong, Tom Fox, Ricardo Pellafone, Nick and Gio Gallo, Tony Charles, Eric Lochner, Ellen Hunt, Mary Shirley, Danette Joslyn-Gaul, Roy Snell, Angelika Flamm, Laura Ellis, and Ben DiPietro.

Thank you to the current and past Sparkies – Diana Trevley, Marnie Smilen, Ramsey Kazem, Nicole Di Schino – and to Sparkies yet unknown. I can't imagine doing this without you.

Thank you to my besties Natalie Leon Walsh and Marnie Smilen. Your support over the last 20-plus years has meant so much to me. I'm so lucky to have you both. Thank you also to Sarah Powell. You've been a rock.

And lastly – this book is dedicated to Lisa Hall and Megan Tepper. The day I shakily proclaimed that I wanted to quit my job to start Spark Compliance, your clamorous cheering propelled me to take the leap. Nothing would have been the same without you.

Kirsten Liston

So many people shaped my career, set amazing examples, and played strong mentorship roles as I grew from aspiring journalist to compliance writer to entrepreneur and company leader.

I have to start by thanking Steve Kaplan, Bill White, and Adam Wahlberg, who gave this intern (turned writer, turned special sections editor) her first professional writing assignments and a place on the masthead at *Minnesota Law & Politics Magazine*. They started me on the path of writing about the law, taught me that nearly any subject that involved people could be fun and interesting, and gave me an indelible picture of three leaders who genuinely enjoyed working together to build something special.

Next, the all-star leadership team at Integrity Interactive, which I was lucky to join as it was just getting off the ground. From Kirk Jordan, who taught me everything I know about successfully leading clients through complex compliance projects, to Carl Nelson, who steered the ship with equanimity and good cheer, to Russell Gee, who could read people better than anyone I've met since, to Sue Jarvi, who set and modeled our service standards and had a talent for mentoring people early in their careers, and to Joe Murphy, who generously shared his compliance expertise and taught ballroom dance lessons at company holiday parties, this formidable team gave me a front row seat during the compliance industry's formative years – thanks to them, I got a world-class education in both compliance and entrepreneurship.

These same people have been unfailingly generous with insights, advice, recommendations, interest, and support as I built Rethink, starting when I called Kirk from a London conference room to say I was thinking about leaving my job to start a company.

My husband Ned is a brilliant business thinker and hiring coach and our work together on the condo business had me thinking like a business owner many years before Rethink was even a possibility. My parents both set an inspiring example with their work ethic and talent for building things from scratch – my dad, who showed me how a high-school dropout could transform himself into a theology professor; my mom, who could organize and improve anything and programmed computer mainframes for some of the biggest companies in the Chicago area (she worked so many hours they named the overtime award after her). And my friend and fellow entrepreneur Jenna Blum has been a cheerleader for my writing since I first took her short story class at Grub Street in Boston in 2003.

To the team at Rethink, including my fellow leaders Patti, Andrea, Tricia, and Matt: I am so proud of what we have built together. What a joy to be associated with such a stellar lineup of A-players, people who set a shared vision for excellence and then work together to make it a reality again and again.

Finally, to Joe and Kristy: Thank you for going on this book-writing journey with me. I have learned so much from you both and have truly enjoyed our collaboration!

Joe Murphy

There are many good things about being in a field for 40 years. But one difficult thing is that there are just too many people who have helped, inspired, and guided me on this journey. And as I explained to Kristy and Kirsten, in decades of writing books and articles I had not been asked before to do an acknowledgement. Dedications, yes, but never anything like this. I am a big believer in thanking people, and I have tried to do that at each stage of my career.

So I would like to do something a bit unusual. I would like to acknowledge three people who will likely never see this acknowledgement, never even know about this book, and may never have known that they played a role in the development of this field. They are three managers I knew from my first days as a young lawyer helping managers who were in the unusual position of being liaisons and champions for the company's competitors – competitors who everyone else in the company viewed as most unwelcome.

One was George Glass, also known as "Mr. Clean." He was the contact for those who competed with Bell on customer telephone equipment. For every customer they had, they needed to deal with Bell, their competitor. Mr. Clean was their doorway and their champion. I was his in-house lawyer.

Then there was Dan Francesky, the general trade guy. If a supplier wanted to sell us switching or other equipment, they had to compete with the in-house suppler, Western Electric. Dan had to be their champion and the one who pushed in-house purchasers to be fair to all suppliers. I was his in-house lawyer.

Finally, there was the Bell point of contact (BPOC) that was the liaison for new, competitive long-distance companies that competed with AT&T. Like the equipment competitors, they could not reach their customers without going through Bell. BPOC managers worked with company people to be sure these competitors could get through. I was their in-house lawyer, including for their manager, Ed Lowry.

Thank you to the many people who have helped me, and thanks for those early clients who taught me that people inside a company could stand up for what they knew was right, and deserved all the support we could give them.

ABOUT THE AUTHORS

Kristy Grant-Hart is an expert in designing and implementing effective international compliance programs for multi-national companies. She is a professional speaker, author, former professor, and thought leader in the compliance profession. She is the founder and CEO of Spark Compliance Consulting, an international consulting company specializing in pragmatic, proportionate, and pro-business compliance and ethics solutions. She is also the creator of the Compliance Competitor game and other compliance-related software and training products.

Mrs. Grant-Hart formerly served as Chief Compliance Officer for United International Pictures, the joint distribution company for Paramount Pictures and Universal Pictures, based in London. While there, she was shortlisted for the Chief Compliance Officer of the Year award at the Women in Compliance Awards.

Mrs. Grant-Hart was an Adjunct Professor at Delaware School of Law, Widener University teaching Global Compliance and Ethics to Masters of Jurisprudence students. Mrs. Grant-Hart began her legal career at the international law firm of Gibson, Dunn & Crutcher, where she worked in the firm's Los Angeles and London offices.

Mrs. Grant-Hart graduated summa cum laude from Loyola Law School in California. She holds certification as a Corporate Compliance and Ethics Professional – International (CCEP-I) and is a member of the California Bar.

She lives in California with her husband and beloved rescue dogs, Samuel and Mr. Fox.

Kirsten Liston first joined the compliance industry in 2000. Since then, she has worked with leading Fortune 500 and Global 2000 companies to design, develop, and implement global training and communications programs that reduce compliance, ethics, and reputational risk. She is the author of the 2019 book "Creating Great Compliance Training in a Digital World: How to Reach and Persuade Your Audience."

In 2015, Ms. Liston founded Rethink Compliance with a single goal: Use modern tools and communications strategies to create products that truly capture attention and drive behavior and culture change in large global organizations.

Ms. Liston has extensive experience creating materials to address a wide variety of compliance topics, from industry-specific concerns in pharmaceutical, automotive, and consumer products businesses to general corporate compliance topics like competition law, anti-bribery, privacy, and respect. She and her team have written many dozen Codes of Conduct, including in innovative digital formats, and specialize in taking about compliance subjects in an engaging way to digitally-savvy audiences.

She is a former journalist, writing for *Minnesota Law & Politics and Super Lawyers*. Her articles have been published in *Compliance & Ethics Magazine, Compliance and Ethics Professional Magazine, Compliance Week, Ethikos,* and Directors and Boards. She is a frequent speaker at industry conferences, including events hosted by *Compliance Week*, Ethisphere, the Ethics and Compliance Officer Association (ECOA), and the Society for Corporate Compliance and Ethics (SCCE).

She lives outside of Denver with her husband, Ned, and their St. Pyrenees, Clementine.

Joe Murphy's career in organizational compliance and ethics spans four decades and six continents. Known as "The Godfather of Compliance," a pioneer of his profession and an international proponent of his field, Joe has worked with a wide spectrum of private, public, governmental, academic and non-profit entities. He is a Certified Compliance & Ethics Professional and a former member of the board of the Society of Corporate Compliance & Ethics.

Joe is author or co-author of six books on compliance and ethics, including the first one written about the profession. Joe has published more than 100 articles, given over 200 presentations in 21 countries and has been quoted by such publications and news media as the Wall Street Journal, National Law Journal, ABA Journal, CNBC, and Compliance News (Australia).

He is Editor in Chief of SCCE's *Compliance and Ethics Professional Magazine*, the SCCE's Director of Public Policy (pro bono) and an advisor to the Compliance and Ethics Committee of the ABA's Antitrust Section. In 2014, The National Law Journal named Joe one of the 50 Governance, Risk and Compliance Trailblazers and Pioneers. He was recognized in 2005 by the SCCE with its Compliance and Ethics Award.

He has represented SCCE as a consultative partner to the OECD's Working Group on Bribery in Paris, and testified before the US Sentencing Commission on proposed revisions to the Sentencing Guidelines compliance program standards. He currently serves as chair of the advisory board of the Rutgers Center for Government Compliance and Ethics.

Joe has his BA from Rutgers University and his law degree from the University of Pennsylvania.

Joe is also an enthusiastic volunteer with historical and arts organizations in his hometown of Haddonfield, NJ. He is a member of the board of the Community Foundation of South Jersey. Joe has combined his decades-long career with his passion for ballroom dance (and his sense of humor) through the creation of the "Society of Dancing Compliance & Ethics Professionals

Notes

[1] Kristy Grant-Hart, How to Be a Wildly Effective Compliance Officer (Brentham House Publishing Co. 2016).

[2] Noah Wasserman, The Founder's Dilemmas: Anticipating and Avoiding the Pitfalls That Can Sink a Start-Up (Princeton University Press 2013).

[3] T. Harv Eker, Secrets of the Millionaire Mind (HarperCollins 2005).

[4] Joseph Curtis, The 5 Things All Great Salespeople Do (Harvard Business Review

[5] David Maister, Managing the Professional Service Firm (Free Press 1993).

[6] Joseph E. Murphy, A Compliance & Ethics Program on a Dollar a Day: How Small Companies Can Have Effective Programs (SCCE 2010) http://www.corporatecompliance.org/Portals/0/PDFs/Resources/Resource Overview/CEProgramDollarADay-Murphy.pdf

[7] Kirsten Liston, Creating Great Training in a Digital World (SCCE 2019).

[8] Joseph E. Murphy, 501 Ideas for Your Compliance and Ethics Program (SCCE 2008).

[9] Peep Laja, First Impressions Matter: Why Great Visual Design Is Essential (CXL April 20, 2019), https://cxl.com/blog/first-impressions-matter-the-importance-of-great-visual-design/. [referencing https://dejanmarketing.com/media/pdf/credibility-online.pdf].

[10] United States Sentencing Commission, Guidelines Material (2018) https://guidelines.ussc.gov/gl/%C2%A78B2.1.

[11] Organisation for Economic Co-Operation and Development, Recommendation of the Council for Further Combating Bribery of Foreign Public Officials in International Business Transactions, Appendix II, http://www.oecd.org/daf/anti-bribery/44884389.pdf.

[12] Joey Rondazzo, Entrepreneur Mental Health Statistics: The Numbers Don't Lie (Overcoming the Mind, undated) https://overcomingthemind.com/entrepreneur-mental-health-statistics/ [referencing https://cmha.ca/news/entrepreneurs-and-mental-health-study].